Success Begins
at Home

Success Begins at Home

**Educational Foundations
for Preschoolers**

Avima D. Lombard
The Hebrew University
of Jerusalem

127529

Lexington Books
D.C. Heath and Company
Lexington, Massachusetts
Toronto

To Ethan, Tami,
and John

Library of Congress Cataloging in Publication Data

Lombard, Avima
    Success begins at home.

    Includes index.
    1. Socially handicapped children—Education (Preschool)—Israel.
    2. Domestic education—Israel. I. Title.
LC4097.17L65   371.96 '7   81-8355
ISBN 0-669-04798-8   AACR2

Published simultaneously in Canada

Printed in the United States of America

International Standard Book Number: 0-669-04798-8

Library of Congress Catalog Card Number: 81-8355

Contents

List of Figures
and Tables

Foreword

This book is about HIPPY—the Israeli "Home Instruction Program for Preschool Youngsters." This nationally administered home-based program of early childhood education was instigated by the National Council of Jewish Women (NCJW) in 1969. It began as a field experiment in Tel Aviv with 100 four-year-old children. In 1975, following five years of field trials that were repeatedly modified in response to observed problems and formal evaluations, it was adopted for public funding by the newly organized Welfare Program of the Ministry of Education of Israel. By 1980, it was serving children in their fifth, sixth, and seventh years in 12,000 families in eighty communities of the state of Israel. This book describes the social conditions that called for such a program, the theory and planning behind the program, the program's operation, and the results that have been determined thus far by the ongoing evaluation component of the program.

Israel and the United States have both attempted to correct the source of political discontent and friction within ethnic groups attributed to their differing economic productivity and security, which have been strongly correlated with disparate levels of education in those groups. Programs in both countries aim to improve the future of the socioeconomically unsuccessful groups by improving their young children's level of educational achievement. In the United States, this public effort became part of the "War on Poverty," which was instituted by Presidents Kennedy and Johnson when reviews of the evidence of plasticity in early child development made the opportunity for educational experiences during the preschool years tantamount to the ethic of "equality of opportunity" established by the U.S. Constitution (see G.Y. Steiner, *The Children's Cause,* Washington, D.C.: Brookings Institution, 1976).

Israel's idealistic first immigrants brought with them from Europe a well-established parental concern for early learning in the home that had survived despite the oppression and poverty of the Jewish ghettos of Eastern Europe. By 1960, immigration had nearly tripled the Jewish population of the state of Israel, which was established in 1948. Moreover, immigrants from the Islamic countries of Asia and North Africa numbered three times those from Europe. They brought with them high hopes for an economic and political equality denied them in their Islamic countries of origin. Unfortunately, they came with such an inadequate level of education that their children failed to profit from the kindergartens that the better-educated pioneers from European countries had established as part of the state-supported system of education. Because these immigrants from Islamic countries were fellow Jews, those from Europe were less inclined to blame their educational inadequacies on inferior heredity than were better-

educated people of the United States before World War II. It may also be
worth noting here that these immigrants from Asia and North Africa were the
descendants of the Sephardic Jews who, a thousand years earlier, had complained of the low level of education among their Ashkenazi, Yiddish-speaking
brethern of Eastern Europe.

This social history combined with the failure of Israeli kindergartens to
cope effectively with the educational inadequacies of the children of the immigrants from Islamic countries led the NCJW (U.S.A.) Research Institute for
Innovation in Education at the Hebrew University in Jerusalem to seek a means
of improving the educational effectiveness of these immigrant families, focusing on the mothers as the most likely teachers. Thus, where the state-supported
program of early education in the United States, epitomized in Project Head
Start, consisted of earlier schooling, that in Israel (epitomized in HIPPY) has
returned to the family for early education.

Enticing these immigrant mothers from Islamic countries to become the
teachers of their young children was no easy task. An overwhelming majority
considered themselves unqualified. They felt unable to cope with written
materials because nearly half of them were illiterate. In HIPPY, Dr. Avima
Lombard has devised a means of simplifying the mother's task. She has used
role playing during weekly visits from the local aide, typically a neighbor
chosen for this paraprofessional role by a local coordinator. The coordinator,
in turn, taught the local aides in weekly meetings to conduct role playing as a
means of teaching the mothers how to teach. Many of the ideas for HIPPY
were obtained from existing literature and then tested with Israeli mothers
and modified as need was indicated by field observations. For instance, when
the evaluative studies showed that home visits alone failed to improve
mothers' images of themselves as teachers of their young, the program was
changed to incorporate group meetings for the mothers at a place within
walking distance.

Although in some ways HIPPY resembles Project Head Start, HIPPY has
followed the findings from research on compensatory education in the United
States more faithfully than has Project Head Start. Because these findings indicated that the more highly structured the learning materials, the better the
learning, the Research Institute chose programmed instruction for HIPPY as the
teaching technique most likely to maximize success. Project Head Start favored
local autonomy and parent involvement. Therefore, many of those in leadership positions knew little or nothing about the findings from research, and
those who did often refused to accept them. In HIPPY, however, programmed
instruction was combined, at least loosely, with the hierarchical conception of
early psychological development. Direct influence from such European in-
vestigators as Vigotsky and Werner is evident as is some indirect influence from
Piaget. The programmed activities progressed in simple planned stages that
four year olds could readily master, and they advanced to increasing levels of

development or difficulty. With this approach, the "short attention span of young children was no handicap." Missing here is an appreciation of the fact that the short attention span holds only for activities prescribed by others, yet progress was observed to bring the satisfaction of a "feeling of mastery" to the children and to the mothers as they saw their children learning.

The mothers were taught to teach by means of role playing each programmed lesson with the local aides during their home visits. One determinant of a mother's interest in the materials to be learned was her appreciation that they would lead to the success of her child in school. Had there been evidence of the value of mothers' imitating the cooings and babblings of their infants to facilitate the development of vocal imitation and through it language acquisition, an approach that capitalizes on the intrinsic motivation of infants might have been easier to teach the mothers. This might have produced even greater educational gains, but it might also have been harder for the mothers to appreciate that such an approach would lead to the success of their children in school.

The content of the HIPPY teaching materials focuses on three broad cognitive domains: language, discrimination skills, and problem solving. The language instruction focuses on the concept *book* and leads progressively to a growing understanding of all the factors that "go into the creation and reading of a book." Because many of the mothers were illiterate or nearly so, no prior knowledge of or skill in the use of books was assumed, and even such details as "sit next to your child," "open the book to page ____," and "hold the book so that both you and your child can see the page" were included in the early instructions to be role played by the mothers with their local aides.

Even though verbal feedback is a fundamental requirement for verbal interaction, the HIPPY plan excluded the possibility of guiding mothers to any corrective feedback. The mothers were instructed through the role playing to wait for their child's response and then, no matter what the response, to give only the correct answer. Thus, the HIPPY program avoided the Bereiter-Engelmann use of the negative ("This is *not* a ball."). In the verbal interaction, the children's responses varied with four different levels of development: doing, responding, testing, and structuring.

Three categories of concepts were emphasized throughout the program: attributes, spatial relationships, and quantities. Within these categories, the children were taught the elementary abstractions of colors, shapes, positions, and numbers, and these are areas in which Head Start children have been shown to be markedly less proficient than nursery-school children from middle-class families. The program and the program instruction for each of these three domains of content are described in chapter 3.

During the three years of age covered by the HIPPY program, the fifth, sixth, and seventh years, emphasis given to the three major cognitive areas progresses. During the first year, the focus is on the labeling aspect of language and discrimination skills. During the second year, the emphasis on these decreases somewhat and that on problem-solving activities increases. During the third year, the emphasis moves largely to problem solving, and this element is introduced even into the book-based activities.

Although the teaching activities and materials were weighed first in terms of relevance to educational objectives, actual inclusion depended on whether the children enjoyed an activity and would stay with it. The overriding objective in HIPPY was to bring children to the point where they learned to enjoy learning. Another goal was minimizing costs. Even though a combination of weekly home visits and group meetings is expensive in terms of available manpower and money, "remedial teaching for only *one* year costs 40 percent more than *three* years of HIPPY."

Chapter 4 tells the story of the 161 children in the two phases of the original Tel Aviv study (1969-1972). It gives the demographic information about the families of these children, describes the general procedure of teaching and evaluation, and follows the children through the second grade. When they are finished with the second grade, those children who participated in HIPPY for two or more years scored significantly higher on tests of proficiency in reading and arithmetic than did all the children who had had no home instruction, even though some had participated in teacher-instructed pre-kindergarten during their fifth year. Chapter 4 also describes the replication, albeit with modifications, of the Tel Aviv study in Jerusalem (1971-1975). Approximately one-quarter of the children in the Jerusalem sample were less than forty-five months old, and they had difficulty responding to the HIPPY materials. When the tests in reading and arithmetic achievement were repeated at the end of second grade, those children who had experienced the HIPPY program performed better than the controls in both domains. Moreover, teacher assessments indicated that those who experienced the HIPPY program were significantly better in reading and writing and better, but not significantly, in arithmetic, science, and expression.

When the Ministry of Education adopted HIPPY for national implementation in 1975, they requested that its implementation be accompanied by an independent, ongoing study of the effects of the program on children. Chapter 5 tells the story of this implementation and presents the results of the evaluation. Comparison of children's performance on academic achievement tests at the end of second grade shows that the scores of control children in both reading and math had improved over the years, but the HIPPY children in the implementation for which many new community coordinators had to be selected and trained fell short of the level attained by those in the original pilot study. Thus, while HIPPY's impact on this larger sample of children is smaller, evidence that it does exist appears in higher arithmetic scores and reading competency equal to that of older siblings.

Chapter 6 describes the impact of the HIPPY program on the mothers and on those who served as aides and local coordinators. Some of these data were recorded by the coordintors in their monthly or annual reports, and others were gathered by graduate students in the School of Education at the Hebrew University in Jerusalem. These students observed, interviewed, and tested the mothers and aides from time to time in specific areas of interest to the students. While such "data are admittedly 'soft'," approximately 70 percent of the illiterate mothers felt themselves incapable of dealing with such a program as HIPPY even when they were offered help, but the remaining 30 percent used their ingenuity to find ways to remember what had to be done in order to teach their children. Having other children younger than four years old also mitigated against mothers' accepting the invitation to participate. Disorganized family functioning turned out to be the prime cause of dropping out of the HIPPY program after accepting an invitation to participate. Because one study indicated that mothers who drop out early undergo a serious drop in self-esteem that may last two years or more, the local coordinators learned to recognize the signs of families in crises and excluded them from the program in order to help them avoid yet another source of stress.

For those mothers who remain in the HIPPY program, it becomes, as expected, a source of satisfaction and of greater self-esteem to see positive changes in their children's level of performance. Among the clearest signs of change in these mothers was increased interest in furthering their own education. In one town, over 50 percent of the students who enrolled in evening classes for basic education were HIPPY mothers. Also, the children generally expressed joy in seeing their mothers learning and knowing new things.

The teaching aides and local coordinators remarked about their own new sense of social competence and ability to deal with unusual situations. They reported satisfaction in making a contribution to their neighborhoods, in making new friends, and sometimes finding that their husbands recognized their progress by beginning to help out around the house.

Chapter 7 describes a field study undertaken by Chava Cohen of the Research Institute in the winter of 1978 to examine how HIPPY was actually being implemented after several years and to identify any substantive changes that might have taken place in the broader implementation of the original program. Cohen's findings suggest that several factors contribute to the stability and replicability of HIPPY: (1) the organizational structure, the lines of communication, and the known elements in the program such as the activities and materials; (2) a belief in the efficacy of the materials; (3) a sense of mission; (4) successful administration; (5) feedback indicating gratitude on the part of participants; and (6) the sense of a "HIPPY family" which provides cohesiveness and stimulates loyalty. Another finding concerned the importance of interpersonal skills and experience in the success of newly recruited local coordinators.

In chapter 8, Dr. Lombard examines the feasibility of HIPPY, summarizes the main features of the program, and then examines them in terms of recently published findings concerned with the implementation of innovative educational programs. Her book can be read with interest and profit by anyone concerned with early education. Even though the program was developed in response to social conditions within Israel, it has interesting implications for those concerned with early education throughout the world.

J. McVicker Hunt
University of Illinois at Urbana-Champaign

Acknowledgments

A project such as HIPPY is the product of the best efforts and devoted attention of many people. Over the years we have drawn on the good will, talents, and skills of students, teachers, and field workers too numerous to name, but to whom I owe many thanks. Thanks are also due to the participants: the coordinators, the aides, and especially the mothers, whose enthusiasm and cooperation make our task an ongoing pleasure.

I am particularly grateful to Abraham Tannenbaum, who provided the original model for the project and guided us in the crucial early years of program development; and to Helene Levy, Hava Cohen, and Carmen Sabagh, who blended creativity and systematic orderliness in preparing the program materials that continue to provide enjoyment and learning for thousands of children.

In the processes of program production, data gathering, program review, and revisions, we were ably assisted by Orly Safrabi, Naomi Paynton, Bina Bresser, Paula Silberstein, Kari Druck, Laura Levine, and Amal Gafil. Their involvement, devotion, and insightful contributions to the research and development of HIPPY were of immeasurable help.

The skillful transformation of our experiment into a viable nationwide program has been the unique contribution of Sara Lior, working with Joseph Benvenisti, Yair Levin, and Shlomo Ben Eliyahu. I am indebted to them for their dedication to the task and their adherence to the essential ideas that constitute the core of HIPPY.

I am grateful to the National Council of Jewish Women (NCJW) in the United States, whose ongoing support has made possible the continued growth and development of HIPPY, and to the National Council of Jewish Women of Canada, who provided the funds for the original study. My thanks also go to my colleagues at the School of Education and the NCJW (U.S.A.) Research Institute for Innovation in Education, Seymour Fox, Dan Davis, and Jane Cohen, who provided help and support at every stage; and to Leah Adar for her valuable comments and suggestions for the final version of the manuscript.

The writing of this book was made possible by a grant provided by the Ford Foundation. For the final manuscript I am indebted to Kaye Weinberger and Norma Schneider, whose comprehensive and painstaking help in writing, organizing, and editing brought it to fruition.

Finally, I would like to give special thanks to my colleague and friend, Chaim Adler, whose encouragement, support, and guidance over the years gave impetus to the growth of HIPPY and the writing of this book. It has been his dream, now shared by us all, that the HIPPY experience be made available to mothers and children around the world. This book is a first step in that direction.

Success Begins
at Home

1

The Setting for a Home Intervention Program

Western societies have been increasingly concerned about the disparate achievement level of various groups in the society. No one expects to find total equality among people and groups, but a problem for all groups arises when any one group of people consistently fails to master its environment, insofar as economic security and the ability this allows them to determine the way in which they will live their lives are concerned.

The gap between successful and unsuccessful socioeconomic groups has become a growing source of discontent and friction. Legislators and concerned professionals have devoted much time and money to the search for means of closing that gap. Not all of these attempts have yielded positive results, and some have yielded none. Nonetheless a body of knowledge relating to the nature of the gap itself, the nature of the population involved, and the dynamics of intervention relating to these factors has been accumulating during the process of seeking solutions. This body of knowledge suggests an interrelationship between educational achievement and socioeconomic status. Whereas not all who fail in education fail later in life, a disproportionately high percentage of those who do fail in the social and economic spheres suffered their earliest failure in the educational establishment (Clark 1962; Hess and Shipman 1968; Passow and Elliott 1968; Plowden 1967; Jencks et al. 1973).

For this reason, efforts to improve the lot of the socioeconomically unsuccessful in our society frequently have focused on finding a way to improve the level of school achievement among young children. Over the past few decades, public funds and professional energies have been expended in an effort to prevent future failure by maximizing the educational potential of young children.

The case for early intervention is based both on a general belief in the effectiveness of early childhood education and on a growing body of data indicating the effectiveness of such educational programs for young disadvantaged children. Both social and educational considerations have brought about dramatic increases in the provision of supervised group care for toddlers and older preschool children. The changing status of women has been a force in creating the need for group care of young children, and this, in turn, has refocused attention on the effect of early experiences on the child's later performance (Bronfenbrenner 1974; Madden et al. 1976; Lazar et al. 1977).

1

In the case of well-functioning middle-class children, the question is whether children are held back in their emotional, intellectual, or social growth by being away from their mothers during these important early years. But with regard to children raised in socially and economically depressed areas, the question is whether they can benefit from the enrichment program offered by day-care centers or similar settings. In both cases the underlying assumption is that these early years are critical. And in both cases it is assumed that the home and the family provide a singular contribution to the educational development of young children during their early years.

There is nothing unusual in this last assumption, especially since children are socialized in the family, which provides their earliest educational setting. The process of education in the family is multidimensional and multidirectional:

> Like any educational institution, the family originates some educative efforts, mediates others, and actually insulates its members from still others. What is more, educative efforts within a family involve not only parents teaching children but children teaching parents, parents teaching one another, and children teaching one another. [Cremin 1974, p. 85]

The family educational setting, however, can prove nonproductive for the child. One such situation occurs when what a child learns from the home situation is at variance with how he or she is expected to act in the school setting.

> Other children have experienced primarily a survival or subsistence rather than an achievement ethic, with consequent high valuation on the present rather than the future, on immediate rather than deferred gratification, on concrete rather than symbolic commitment. Where these children live hardly anyone ever gets to the top; often one cannot even move across the street. Time is not important or potentially valuable if there is not going to be anything to do with it anyway. And what does an appeal to symbolic success mean where success can be measured realistically only by substance and survival? These children, in contrast to other children, face severe discontinuities in values when they come to school—discontinuities often having a profound effect on their behavior toward school and the school's behavior toward them. [Getzels 1974, p. 45]

The strength of the relationship between home environment and school performance has been systematically documented again and again over the past fifteen years. Coleman's (1966) conclusion that "the school appears unable to exert independent influences to make achievement levels less dependent on the child's background" (p. 297) provided early confirmation of what had previously been a hunch rather than a substantiated finding. Subsequent research found that aspects of the home environment (Garber and Ware 1972), child-rearing practices (Barton et al. 1974), and the degree to which education is valued in the home (Gross 1970) were among the predictors of school achievement.

The verbal interaction patterns and language forms used between parents and children were found to be related to school success by Bernstein (1961), Jones (1972), and Radin (1974). Swan and Stavros (1973), in their search for child-rearing practices that determine adequate learning patterns, found that the characteristics that are the best predictors are those that usually describe well-functioning middle-class families. In these families, the parents maintain a helpful and encouraging attitude toward their child's being an adventurous, creative, and independent learner. Such parents also tend to use more open and fewer closed questions in conversing with their children, a style of questioning that produces a greater quantity of verbal response from the children (Paynton 1972).

Other researchers have focused on identifying those behaviors that seem to characterize mothers of disadvantaged children. Hess and Shipman (1965) found that these mothers provide neither the necessary information nor the rationale for problem solving to their children. They tend to use more punitive, controlling, and irritable behaviors (Bayley and Schaefer 1960). Middle-class mothers tend to concentrate more on encouraging their children to tasks and to use more positive control and reinforcement strategies, more praise, and less criticism and to intrude less into their children's tasks (Brophy 1970; Olmsted and Jester 1972; Bee et al. 1969; Feshbach 1973).

As the United States was awakening to and showing interest in the needs of the disadvantaged, similar issues were also coming to the fore in Israel. The early years of Israel's statehood (1948-1960) were characterized by waves of mass immigration from Europe, America, Asia, and North Africa, which almost tripled the Jewish population in the first twelve years of the state (see table 1-1) and radically altered its composition. Shuval's 1963 breakdown of immigration over the first three years of statehood shows the following shift in ethnic composition during these years: the proportion of immigrants from Asia increased from 5 percent in 1948 to 34.4 percent in 1950; from Africa, from 9 percent to 15.2 percent; from Europe it decreased from 85 percent to just under 50 percent.

Over half the immigrants during this period came from the Islamic countries of the Middle East and North Africa, with social and economic circumstances, as well as cultural traditions, that were in sharp contrast to those of the veteran indigenous population that had forged the social and political foundations of the state of Israel and who were mainly from Europe.

A number of characteristics distinguished the Afro-Asian group. The immigrants from these countries tended to have large numbers of children,

Table 1-1
Jewish Immigration, by Period of Immigration and Continent of Birth

Year	Africa and Asia		Europe and North America		Total	
	Percent	N	Percent	N	Percent	N
1919-1948	10.4	44,809	89.6	385,066	100.0	429,875
1948-1950[a]	40.5	207,209	55.8	285,528	96.3	511,610
1951-1953[a]	67.2	141,712	29.2	61,539	96.4	210,824
1954-1956	87.8	98,365	12.2	13,692	100.0	112,082
1957-1959[a]	40.7	49,775	58.8	71,816	99.5	122,201
1960-1962	57.8	77,097	42.2	56,363	100.0	133,476
1963-1965	54.0	80,969	46.0	68,843	100.0	149,816
1966-1968	58.4	29,539	41.6	21,056	100.0	50,601
1969-1977[a]	20.3	65,185	79.3	254,176	99.6	320,448

Source: Central Bureau of Statistics, *Statistical Abstract of Israel,* no. 29 (1978), p. 137.
[a]In this period there was a small percentage of immigrants whose country of origin was unknown.

to emphasize kinship ties, to regard the extended rather than the nuclear family as a social unit, and often to live together in such units. Their rather rigid tendency to hand down occupations from father to son, with little or no vocational specialization, resulted in their concentration in small businesses and crafts, with minimum flow to the technical occupations and professions (Eisenstadt 1955, 1956; Shuval 1963; Minkovich, Davis, and Bashi 1977).

In the sphere of education, this group of immigrants was at a distinct disadvantage. Illiteracy was not uncommon, particularly among the women who had few if any years of formal schooling. Minkovich et al. (1977) describe the general level of education of the Afro-Asian immigrants as "woefully inadequate" (p. 15), assessing their illiteracy at 40 percent. Figures for 1961 cited by Inbar and Adler (1977) indicate that 34.4 percent of the Moroccans in Israel over the age of fourteen had no schooling whatsoever. This figure represents 46.7 percent of the women and 23.1 percent of the men, further evidence that the problem was far greater for women.

The mass influx of Afro-Asian immigrants was expressive of religious and nationalist ideology and, perhaps even more significant for this group, of the desire for the political and economic equality with its attendant promise of upward social mobility denied them in their countries of origin (Shuval 1963). A number of factors, however, combined to frustrate their realization of these desires. The state of Israel was then in the process of emerging from the struggles of its war for independence. Its highly precarious economic and security situation left it unprepared and for the most part unable to absorb such vast numbers of immigrants adequately; it lacked both the infrastructure and the economic capacity for the task. The absorption difficulties of the Afro-Asian immigrants were compounded by their inherent educational and occupational limitations, their poor economic circumstances (aggravated in many instances by having to leave their possessions behind), the language barrier, and a cultural background at odds with that of the European veterans. In addition, the problems of some groups, the Moroccans for instance, were exacerbated by the fact that the indigenous elite was not included in the wave of immigration; this increased their dependency on the absorptive society.

Faced with a severe housing shortage, the government generally directed immigrants to transit camps. Intended as a temporary solution, the period of residence often stretched into years for these immigrants. The fact that the transit camps were usually located in areas isolated from the mainstream of Israeli life severely limited occupational opportunities.

The unsettling effects of such temporary surroundings on the immigrants led the government to adopt a policy of population dispersal that resulted in a new form of settlement, the development town. Each such town located in undeveloped regions around the country, and planned around local industry and service needs, was designed to become an independently functioning community. A large proportion of Afro-Asian immigrants were moved to these towns and became their almost exclusive inhabitants. Although the population dispersal policy may have been necessary for the state, it was detrimental to the Afro-Asian immigrants because it concentrated them in certain industries and limited the occupational opportunities available to them (Spilerman and Habib 1976). Their traditional occupations did not equip them for the manual and technical jobs offered in the towns, and their lack of formal education stood in the way of occupational retraining, thereby frustrating their desires and expectations for rapid social mobility. Furthermore their inability to use the democratic process to run their own affairs, born in part of lack of experience, did nothing to enhance their image as a group. The consequent imposition of an outsider, often of European origin, to administer community affairs added to this aspect of the problem.

The immigrants from this group who ventured to the cities did little better. There too they were hampered by the inappropriateness of their skills in a developing society and by their inability to compete on equal terms with the better-educated, more highly skilled veteran population. Thus their hopes and expectations for speedy absorption and financial success could not be quickly gratified. The neighborhoods in the cities, where these Afro-Asian immigrants lived became slums, their inhabitants characterized by generally low educational achievement and low-status jobs.

Despite some quite impressive achievements in the absorption activities carried out over the succeeding years, to a large extent this immigrant group has continued to lag behind the rest of Israeli society. They are unable to break out of the cycle of poverty, poor employment or unemployment, in-adequate housing, and low educational achievement. And they certainly have not taken leadership positions in Israeli society proportionate to their numbers (Minkovich et al. 1977; Smooha 1978).

The children of these immigrant families had few if any of the precondi-tions favorable to educational success. The Israeli school system, although it had a well-established network of high-standard primary education, was unable to cope with extending its facilities to vast numbers of children in a compressed time span. As a result the quality of schools in disadvantaged areas was poor: the buildings tended to be makeshift and unsuited to their purpose, equipment was inadequate in supply and poor in condition, and the quality of the available teaching staff was lower than elsewhere. Few teachers were ready to take on the challenge and responsibility for pupils who presented behavior, learning, and motivational problems.

Not only did the system fail to fulfill the needs of the children of these immigrants, but the immigrants themselves could not cope with the modern, Western-type Israeli school and its European achievement-oriented tradition. The parents' relative unfamiliarity with the Hebrew language, combined with a seemingly unbridgeable cultural gap, precluded effective teacher-parent communication and cooperation. Teachers viewed the parents as not being "education-minded" and as lacking the incentive to become interested in their children's education at any level. The parents, who were themselves poorly educated, had neither the knowledge nor the ability to help their children in the school setting. The generally over-crowded homes lacked the atmosphere and facilities conducive to learning at home. Furthermore parents of large families faced with the competing demands of many children found it extremely difficult to cope with the problems of each child individually. Thus the children of these families were not only ill equipped to meet the expectations of the school system but were further frustrated and handicapped by the limitations imposed on them at home.

By the mid-1950s a number of evaluation procedures brought this educational divide to the attention of the Ministry of Education. In refer-ring to this period, Minkovich et al. (1977, p. 17) point out that "an awareness emerged that Israel had to face the problem of the educationally disadvantaged pupil." Because the concept of equality in education, which had been the basis for educational planning in Israel, did not yield the expected equality in educational outcomes, it was broadened to include the concept of equality of educational opportunity. Extra funds and personnel were expended on the initiation of new programs for disadvantaged children, and a special center was established in the Ministry of Education to deal with the education of disadvantaged children. The new programs undertaken included free prekindergartens for three and four year olds, the extension of the school day in primary school from twenty-four to thirty-two hours per week (the regular school day runs from 8 A.M. to 1 P.M. six days a week), special teacher-training courses, tutorial help for pupils, ability grouping in the primary grades, revision of the curriculum for disadvantaged children, and boarding schools for gifted children from disadvantaged homes (Adiel 1970).

By 1968, when the waves of mass immigration from Islamic countries were stopping, the issue of the educationally disadvantaged had come into clear focus. At this time the National Council of Jewish Women (U.S.A.) established the Research Institute for Innovation in Education at the School of Education of the Hebrew University of Jerusalem dedicated to designing, implementing, and evaluating educational methods, materials, and resources aimed at facilitating the integration of Israel's disadvantaged children and youth into the mainstream of the country's society.

One of the first field projects developed at the new institute focused on the young disadvantaged child. Early education has been well established in Israel since the latter part of the nineteenth century. It has been an integral part of the educational system since the establishment of the state in 1948, when kindergarten was declared part of the free and compulsory school system. Thus there existed in Israel an accepted tradition of early group care and nurturing of children between the ages of three and seven, especially of those in need of community support. The early day-care centers evolved into educational centers as the teachings of Froebel and his followers were adopted locally. The specific aims of these nursery-kindergartens were clear: to teach the Hebrew language and to prepare the children for school:

> These youngsters will no longer come [to school] bereft of all knowledge of reading and writing. In addition, the language spoken in the institution will only be Hebrew, so that when the children reach school they will already speak Hebrew and their teachers will be able to teach all subjects, including the Torah, without translating into another language. [Rinot 1971, p. 80]

In spite of their having recourse to this well-established head start, in 1968 Israeli children of Afro-Asian origin still seemed to be starting first grade with an almost unsurmountable disadvantage. It was quite clear that preschool education by itself could not prepare these children adequately for school.

Despite the fact that the two major educational influences on children are their family and their school, all efforts to ease the disadvantaged child's way into the formal school system had been concentrated within the system itself. Although educators had suggested that the family was responsible for children's lack of school success, it had not yet been the target of intervention. This was not only due to a reluctance to intrude upon the family, undermining its ability to function as a unit, but also to a belief that nothing could help these families and the children would be best served by counteracting family influences as early as possible.

Another serious consideration was the content of any such intervention. In what way and in which direction should change be created in the family of the disadvantaged child? There are basic differences between the families of Israeli disadvantaged children and those of Western countries reported in the literature. The Israeli families are predominantly intact, and the father's position is dominant. Characteristically they believe in education and its potential for changing their lot.

Although an intervention program was therefore expected to be well accepted by the Israeli disadvantaged families, there was relatively little specific information on them that could be of help in setting guidelines for planning intervention. Yet teachers and community workers in contact with these families could identify with certainty those characteristics of life-style and patterns of interaction that were counterproductive to school success. These families lacked books and toys for the children's use, space for play, quiet and private places for doing homework, parental interest in the child as an individual, parental contact with the school and the teachers, and parental assistance with the child's education. Some of these were easily verifiable; others were more elusive. In exploring the lack of parental involvement, we found an overwhelming majority of mothers who said they would not be able to have any effect on their child's education even if they wanted to. They commented "I never learned," "I'm not smart enough to be my child's teacher," "There are people who get special training for that," "They know what to do, that's why I send my child to school. . . . I'll send him as young as you like . . . the younger the better . . . he'll learn there."

Because the kindergarten year had not proved as helpful as had been hoped and because programs for children prior to kindergarten at the time were essentially downgraded kindergarten programs, there was little reason to believe that more and earlier schooling would improve these children's chances of success in school. Moreover, children spent only four or five hours in school each day and the rest of their waking hours with their families. Even the most superior educational institution would find it difficult to counter the effect of the time that these children spent in their noneducation-oriented families. This does not even take into account the fact that the emotional impact of family members on each other is far greater than that of any interactions to be found in the school setting.

This lack of parental awareness of the home as an educational setting does not imply lack of belief in education for their children, however. There is a strong belief among these families that change comes about through education, and since change from the status quo is what they seek, education is high on their scale of values. It has been suggested (Lightfoot 1978) that overly high expectations from the school system may in fact be one of the causes of parental conflict with it, especially when their children do not succeed within the system (that is, the system is failing the parents). Because these parents feel unable to deal with a conflict involving such a powerful system, they become apathetic and detach themselves from it.

At the Research Institute, we thought that our efforts should be directed to the homes of these young children. Maybe we could find a way to bring changes into the home that would help children to be better prepared to deal with the demands of school. In focusing on the home setting, it seemed clear that we would have to consider two major areas: the educational enrichment of the child and strengthening the mother's self-esteem through her activities as an educator in the family setting. Mothers rather than fathers were chosen because they are the ones who most consistently care for and spend time with young children. Fathers generally are around only at bedtime hours and during the one-day Sabbath weekend.

The program that we evolved was HIPPY (Home Instruction Program for Preschool Youngsters), now nationally administered and publicly funded. It was developed by the Research Institute in 1969 as a small field experiment with one hundred children in Tel-Aviv. This number rose to almost five hundred children as HIPPY was introduced into a variety of urban and rural, small and large communities, in the years that followed. By 1975, after having undergone several changes in content and form and after it had proved to be both hardy and effective, HIPPY was adopted by the newly funded Welfare Program of the Ministry of Education. It has grown rapidly since then. Currently over twelve thousand families take part in the national project, representing more than eighty-five communities throughout the country.

2 How HIPPY Works

HIPPY is a home-based enrichment program in which a mother works with her young children from the time they are four until they are six years old on a particular set of educational activities. She receives these materials in weekly packets from a paraprofessional aide, herself a mother of a preschool child and a member of the same community. The aide is selected by a professional coordinator, chosen locally, whose qualifications include higher education and experience in working with mothers and their children. This local coordinator is guided in her work by a regional coordinator, selected by the national administrator of HIPPY from among the local coordinators. The regional coordinator supervises the local coordinators in the twenty to twenty-five locations that make up her region and works in conjunction with the national administrator, based at the Research Institute at the Hebrew University of Jerusalem.

The program is aimed at educationally disadvantaged children. Families selected for the program are of Afro-Asian origin, have a low level of education (fewer than ten years), and fall into the lower ranges of the economic scale. They are generally large, intact families, where five or more children per family are not uncommon, and homes are small, often a total of three rooms or fewer.

A mother who joins HIPPY meets weekly with the paraprofessional aide, who instructs her in how to administer the materials to her child. These weekly meetings alternate between private home visits and group meetings. The aide visits the mother at an appointed time every other week, bringing with her the workbook and packet of materials for that week. She uses role playing to instruct the mother in their use, the aide and the mother taking turns playing the roles of mother and child. This activity ensures that the mother is fully familiar with the materials. When the mother is illiterate or for some other reason unable to cope with written materials alone, an older sibling chosen by the mother assumes the teaching role, and the training session with the aide takes place with this sibling but in the mother's presence. The mother is encouraged to participate to the limit of her abilities since she is the major focus of the program.

In the course of each meeting, there is time to discuss problems concerning both the mother's and the child's participation in the program, such as difficulties with specific activities or the child's lack of concentration. These problems often surface when the aide checks through the previous week's workbook. They may also be raised by the mother.

The national administration of HIPPY incorporates both the Research Institute and the Ministry of Education. The national administrator, a member of the institute staff, works in close cooperation with the budget administrator of the Ministry's Educational Welfare Programs to determine costs, establish guidelines for local administration of the program, and deal with new issues as they arise.

Israel has been divided into four administrative regions, each headed by a HIPPY regional coordinator, who conducts regular visits to all of the programs in her region, sees how each one is working, and helps local coordinators. She conducts regular monthly training sessions for the local coordinators in her region and is responsible for the quality of instruction and administration of their programs.

The regional coordinators are responsible to the national administrator, with whom they meet in Jerusalem monthly. In addition to focusing on administrative and supervisory problems that may have arisen, these meetings provide the national administrator with a small forum in which to discuss new plans and guidelines for HIPPY as it expands around the country.

Since 1975 HIPPY has been fully funded by the Ministry of Education from monies allocated to school districts with high percentages of educationally disadvantaged children. Each school district is allotted a sum of money for enrichment programs by the ministry, which also provides a list of approved projects. The school district then selects the school-community program that best meets local needs.

When HIPPY is the program chosen, the local school district notifies both the Ministry of Education and the Research Institute. The institute sends out guidelines for the selection of local coordinators, and a search for appropriate candidates gets underway in the spring of the year in which the program is to begin. Candidates found suitable by the local authorities are sent to the national administrator who, together with the appropriate regional coordinator, interviews them and selects one person. This selection is final and binding and is accepted by the local school districts because only those candidates approved locally are considered by the national administration.

The local coordinator's role links the administrative and the practical aspects of the program. She serves as liaison between the program and the formal education setting to ensure understanding and cooperation on both sides. When necessary she also creates links between HIPPY families and outside agencies, directing families to the relevant social services. Through her participation in community committees related to projects for parents and children, she publicizes HIPPY, coordinates its activities with other programs, and ensures the cooperation of the various community bodies with the HIPPY program.

The local coordinator makes the initial contacts with the families, collects basic data relating to the family circumstances, and discusses the program with each mother in the home in order to make sure that she understands exactly what is involved before she agrees to join the program. HIPPY requires a mother to allot a certain amount of time each week, preferably on a daily basis, to working through a packet of activities with her child.

When making her first visit to a family, the local coordinator also tries to do an early assessment on the mother as a possible paraprofessional aide and discusses the possibility with her if she believes that the mother would function well in this role. When several possible candidates have been identified, the local and regional coordinators interview them together before final selections are made; one such aide is chosen for every twelve to eighteen families. The local coordinator then holds weekly training sessions with the aides and provides them with ongoing support, advice, and guidance on problems that arise in the course of their work. She comes into direct contact with the families in her area in the biweekly group meetings of mothers and aides and also when visiting the home to observe how the aide is teaching the mother. (She may also be asked by an aide to intervene in certain situations.) The quality of the aide's teaching is of paramount importance because the mother learns the techniques for working with her child from the aide.

Each aide keeps an up-to-date account of the activity packet on which each child under her supervision is currently working and maintains records on all the families in her care: ten to twelve families in the first year, rising to fifteen to eighteen families as she gains experience. (Her salary rises commensurately.)

The aides meet in a weekly group with the local coordinator to review the material themselves, to report and discuss the previous week's work, and to air and share experiences and problems. They refer problems that they feel are outside their sphere of competence to the coordinator. This forum also enables the coordinator to monitor the aides' work and to direct them as necessary.

The aides, like the mothers under their supervision, familiarize themselves with the educational materials through role playing with the local coordinator and with each other. They are provided with each packet a week in advance so as to be able to use the materials with their own children before they deliver them to the mothers in their care.

Each mother who contracts to join HIPPY must commit herself to regular attendance at the biweekly meetings with her aide and the five to ten other mothers in the aide's care and to a minimal token participation fee. At the start of each meeting the aide reviews with the mother the child's work for the previous week, sharing problems with the other mothers from time to time as they arise. In the discussion that follows, mothers may share information on problems and suggest solutions that work from their own experience. The group as a whole then reviews the next week's materials, using the same role-playing technique employed by the aide and mother in the home.

In the second part of the group meeting, which is directed by the local coordinator, several aides and the mothers under their supervision join together in a general educational activity—perhaps a lecture, a demonstration, or an activity relevant to the parental role. Topics, suggested by the aides, the local coordinator, or the mothers, include health and hygiene, children's books and games, the school system, home handicrafts, home economics, and preparation for holidays. The sustained absence of a mother from her group meetings, particularly when combined with her not working steadily with her child at home, may result in her being asked to leave the program, although the aide would expend considerable effort first to help the mother remedy the situation.

The organization and implementation of group meetings with mothers is the responsibility of the local coordinator. The HIPPY program in each community is assigned regular meeting places. It is the coordinator's job to see that the meeting place is ready, to arrange for speakers, discussion topics, and exhibits, and to organize special events such as outings, projects, and parties. She also arranges for the storage of the HIPPY materials and their weekly distribution to the aides. She finds substitutes for aides who are ill and deals with problems concerning the aides' conditions of employment. Her case load increases from 80 families in her first year, to 160 in the second, and to 240 in the third year. Her salary increases commensurately.

Each newly selected local coordinator, along with those who have been in the field for from one to eight years, attends a week-long training and enrichment course during the summer. New coordinators are taught about the program, its materials, its method of operation, and their role in it. The training combines formal lectures, discussions, and workshops with ongoing informal discussions with experienced coordinators. Both frameworks have been found to be important to the new coordinators. The formal framework provides basic information and directives in the most effective, organized way, and the informal part enables each coordinator to seek the information and encouragement she needs in her own way and from experienced coordinators from programs of varying size and structure around the country.

During the year the local coordinators receive training at monthly meetings, conducted by the regional coordinator, where the educational materials to be used for that month are reviewed using a role-playing technique. Issues relating to their work as coordinators are raised and discussed.

These may range from general administrative questions to specific problems with a particular family or with the functioning of an aide. At each monthly meeting the regional coordinator plans a discussion on a topic of general interest, such as working with groups, community resources, or specific content areas of the materials. The regional coordinator generally serves as both resource person and supervisor in these meetings.

Soon after the course, the new local coordinators arrange for visits to all new HIPPY locations by the HIPPY program team: the national administrator, the ministry's budget administrator, the HIPPY regional coordinator, and the newly selected and trained local coordinator. The primary object of these visits is to get the program off to a good start. The local representatives generally include the chairman of the local council (sometimes the mayor), the head of the local department of education, the head of the local community center, and representatives of the department of social welfare. HIPPY is described in detail to all of the local representatives, and all questions relating to its administration and funding are clarified.

The final determination of the specific local neighborhoods in which HIPPY will be initiated is made during this visit. The neighborhoods chosen represent those that have a real need and yet are not the worst in that community so that a stigma will not be attached to the program at its inception. The neighborhood chosen must also have large concentrations of four year olds, as well as appropriate meeting places for mothers and aides, within walking distance of the mothers' homes to make attendance as easy as possible.

Site visits made to the neighborhood establish the appropriateness of the selection and of the meeting places suggested. Having determined the neighborhood and the target nursery schools within it, the potential children can be identified and the local coordinator can set about visiting families to get the program underway.

A community that elects HIPPY as an educational program is committing itself for at least three years, and generally more. Eighty families of four year olds are selected from the target nursery schools for the first year. The following year these children continue in the program as five year olds, and a new group of 80 four-year-old children is selected from the same nursery schools. In the third year, when the original group is six years old, the total grows to 240, as 80 new four year olds are added. A unit of 220 to 240 families is considered complete and can continue functioning as long as there are enough young children in the neighborhood to replace those who complete the program. A community that decides to introduce HIPPY into another neighborhood must treat it as a new program, starting from the beginning with the selection of a local coordinator.

Where there are not enough families of young children to warrant opening an entire new program—for instance, in a development town with only

120 children in any one age group—the local coordinator may agree to expand her group and take on a practical coordinator to assist her. This position is given to an aide who, after working three years or more with the program, has proven to be exceptionally able. This aide assists the local coordinator in administrative tasks, in training new aides, and in the administration of the group meetings with mothers.

3 Considerations in Planning the Program

One of the major pitfalls of any program development is that basically good ideas are very often not thought through. We therefore tried to identify the major areas that had to be taken into consideration in order to ensure that HIPPY would not fail by default.

Three basic questions arose during the planning and development of HIPPY: how to involve the mothers, how to provide the children with attractive and effective home activities, and how to build a program that can work in disadvantaged neighborhoods.

Attracting and Involving Mothers

Because the central theme of our program is the active involvement of the mother in education activities with her child and because our target mothers not only had no previous experience with such activities but had also previously rejected any idea that they were capable of helping their children in this area, a central concern was how to involve them. And once having gained their involvement, how could we keep them engaged for a period long enough to provide a basis for change in both them and their children?

Another problem was that the kinds of activities we would ask the mother to engage in would very likely remind her of her own lack of success in school and in learning situations. Therefore everything possible had to be done to guarantee her success in the program. If she could carry out the activities successfully, her satisfaction would be likely to provide impetus for further involvement. Moreover, if the activity were to produce clearly visible changes in her child's comprehension or ability level, her involvement would acquire high value for her, thereby resulting in additional satisfaction.

Early studies of the various possible modes of instructing young disadvantaged children indicate that the more highly structured the material to be learned, the better the results (Karnes et al. 1970a). Young children can learn a variety of relatively difficult skills through programmed instruction, and Gotkin (1963) found it a singularly appropriate method for teaching young children who had different rates of learning. Keisler and McNeil (1961) found that it was an effective way to teach first-grade children abstract scientific language, and Hively (1962) used it to train both preschool and first-

17

grade children in a series of progressively difficult discrimination tasks. In studies of programmed instruction, the children appeared to be involved, interested, and responsive.

Programmed instruction was therefore the technique that we expected would maximize the probability of success. Everything the mother had to do for each activity was specifically stated; she was required to make no decisions. The HIPPY program of activities was structured to progress in simple, planned stages with the objective of providing children with a series of tasks that they could master easily as they advanced to increasing levels of difficulty. Programmed instruction in the administration of the materials has other benefits: the short attention span of young children is not a handicap in this type of instruction, and it brings about a feeling of mastery in the mother as well as the child because she can see, as her child is learning, that it is she who is bringing about his learning.

We selected role playing as our basic technique for teaching "how to teach" because it has been found to be especially successful for use with the disadvantaged. The emphasis is on action rather than talk; it is down to earth and concrete, and its easy, informal tempo provides a gamelike rather than a test-oriented setting (Riessman 1972). Thus role playing provided a nonthreatening atmosphere in which both mother and aide could clarify specific problems and areas of weakness in the mother's understanding of the materials and how she could deal with them.

In the role-playing situation, each role is clearly delineated at the outset and the circumstances are carefully established since the role-playing responses elicited are not usually within the participants' behavioral repertoire (Sulzer and Mayer 1972). The fact that both mother and aide alternate in assuming the role of mother or child allows the problems and weaknesses to be handled as naturally as possible.

Role playing also provides an opportunity for the mother to learn teaching techniques through modeling. According to Kafner (1973, p. 23), "Under proper conditions individuals can undergo considerable behavior changes by systematic exposure to models. The basic vicarious learning paradigm is one in which a person is given the opportunity to observe a model and is then required to perform the same task as the model." In HIPPY the constraints imposed by the use of paraprofessional aides whose experience in formal or informal educational settings was limited, precluded the possibility of transmitting a set of verbal rules for teaching in a meaningful way. The equivalent of such rules was transmitted from coordinator to aide to mother in the process of observing and practicing the behaviors modeled in situations that closely resemble the mother-child teaching-learning interaction.

The mothers' interest in administering the actual materials was seen to depend on whether they appear to be materials that will lead to the realization of her objectives—the success of her child in school—and whether they are materials that her child could in fact learn and make progress with. Since the HIPPY activities were carefully programmed, there was little doubt that the mother would receive immediate confirmation that her child was learning and progressing. As to the apparent relatedness of the activities to what children do in school, an attempt was made in structuring the program to have each activity meet this criterion. When there was a doubt as to how the mother might view or accept a new activity series, the aides' instructions (also preprogrammed) included simple explanations for the mother as to why they were important for her child's success.

Both the mother's initial willingness to participate in the program and the extent to which she would be willing to remain in the program for the necessary time originally were viewed to be a function of the ease with which she could accomplish that which was asked of her. Thus in addition to providing programmed materials that had a high likelihood of being meaningful to her, the original model for the HIPPY program had the aides visiting the mothers in their homes every week rather than biweekly.

Only three of the forty-eight mothers receiving home instruction dropped out in the first experimental year of the program, thereby strengthening our belief in this system. However, a study involving the population of the HIPPY experiment conducted in the following year at the institute by Davis and Kugelmas (1974) led us to conclude that ease of participation could not be the only criterion of success. The aim of this study was to use the HIPPY research population (experimental and control) to gather information on how disadvantaged parents viewed their contribution to the education of their children. The researchers found indications that, when compared to a control group, mothers in HIPPY tended to value motivation and competence skills, as well as cognitive abilities, over social-emotional capabilities. The authors suggested that the HIPPY mothers "may have learned to look at their children in new, different terms as a result of the project experience" (p. 28).

They found no evidence, however, of any change in the mothers' views of themselves as educators. We learned from the several questions that might have yielded such information that the program appeared to have no effect in this area. The authors suggest that "there was little opportunity for [a mother] to communicate with others besides the paraprofessional about the significance of the program, her reactions or problems, her child's reactions, etc." (Davis and Kugelmas 1974, p. 35). In other words, there was little opportunity, outside of her actual implementation of the programmed activities themselves, for the mother to develop her self-image in the teaching role.

In light of these findings, ease of participation became a less important factor, and the HIPPY model was changed to incorporate group meetings for mothers. We believed that such a forum would enable mothers to share their problems and reactions, to learn from the experiences of others, and to internalize, through active discussion, some of the stated objectives of the program. There was, of course, a risk that requiring mothers to attend group meetings might increase the number of dropouts from the program significantly. Meetings were therefore scheduled on a biweekly basis, with home visits continuing in the alternate weeks. Every attempt was made to have the meeting place as convenient as possible, certainly within walking distance. The dropout rate did increase to 15 percent, a significant rise for HIPPY, but when viewed in the context of other parent-participation programs, this increase was not considered problematic.

One of the main reasons for maintaining the home visits at least twice a month was to give support and guidance to those mothers who were especially weak in reading; these ranged from total illiterates to women whose functional reading level was below that of fourth grade. We had initially questioned whether such mothers could be included in the program, but we decided that any mother who could use the program should be in it. The activities were clearly labeled and illustrated, and there was a great deal of repetition in style of presentation. Mothers could take their time in learning what was expected of them, and even if they were to remember and do only half of what was in the workbooks, it would certainly be more than what they would be doing with their youngsters without HIPPY.

In order to give those weak mothers additional help in the program, an older sibling was frequently recruited to assist the preschool child with the workbook. While in this case the mother was still considered in charge of the home activity, much of the direct instruction was turned over to the older child. This is not an ideal situation, and there were frequent school and other pressures that interfered with the older child's ability to help on a regular basis, but generally this variation of HIPPY worked well enough to enable the inclusion of families who would otherwise have been excluded.

Providing Home Activities

Although any child-oriented program must take the child-appeal factor into consideration, the planning of an enrichment program for children must begin with decisions regarding the content and format of that program.

Content

Since little had been published to date on the various levels of functioning of the four-year-old disadvantaged children with whom we would be dealing, we had to begin by creating a conceptual framework within which the program would be written. Three broad cognitive areas clearly had to be included: language, discrimination skills, and problem solving.

Language: Language is essential for the child's development of communication, concept development, and problem-solving skills. There was no question that language development was likely to be a problem in the lives of our HIPPY children. Bernstein (1961) had clearly documented the lack of verbal elaboration of abstract content and subjective intent in the language patterns of the disadvantaged, and information was slowly gathering on the adverse influence that language styles of the disadvantaged have on their learning abilities (Hunt 1964; John 1964) and reading skills (Gupta 1967). Our task was to determine those aspects of language on which our program would focus.

Books can be considered the basic subject matter of language development in young Western children. The concept "book" includes the growing understanding of all the factors that go into the creation and reading of a book. The use of books with young children requires verbal interaction between the reader and the child. When the reader was the mother, as we expected would mostly be the case in HIPPY, she too would benefit, since she would come into contact with language structure and vocabulary, which would provide new bases for her own use of language. This would, in turn, influence her child's acquisition of language skills. In the course of using books to interact with her child, a variety of skills would be developed: listening, answering questions, talking from the text (reading aloud both descriptive and spoken passages), picture reading, story creation, seriation (what happened first, what next . . .), and vocabulary. These are the skills that were to be incorporated into the program. Each one therefore had to be analyzed so as to enable its structuring into the sequential learning program. Some precede others in the hierarchy of learning tasks; for instance, picture reading comes before seriation, especially when a child's orientation is more visual than auditory.

Our basic orientation in planning both the scope and the specifics of the activities concerning books was the knowledge that the mothers in our program do not normally read stories, buy books, or encourage their young children to use them. Therefore since we assumed no prior knowledge of or skill in the use of books with young children, everything included in the administration of the materials would have to be clearly stated, including such details as: "Sit next to your child," "Open the book to page _____," "Hold the book so that both you and your child can see the page." Such detailed instructions were gradually eliminated as mothers progressed in the program and learned these basic rules.

In addition to the reading of the stories themselves, a variety of activities connected with each story was provided in order to develop language skills further. For example, new words were repeated, and ideas and problems raised in the stories were discussed and used as the basis for games created especially for the purpose. Nonverbal activities such as coloring, cutting, and pasting were programmed into book-related activities, much in the same way as language activities and verbal skills were incorporated into other aspects of the program.

One of the fundamental requirements for verbal interaction as a language-learning experience is the use of verbal feedback. Since the HIPPY model must preclude the possibility of guiding mothers to differential corrective feedback, they were simply told that they must always wait for the child's response and then, no matter what that response, to give only the correct answer. Thus even the child who answers incorrectly or remains silent will hear the correct answer, thereby learning that the first response was incorrect. A child who gives the correct answer receives confirmation of this. The mother-child work sheets are structured to remind both of this rule.

Verbal interaction involves the child as well. Children's responses are varied and at different levels of developmental sophistication. The HIPPY pattern for programming these responses was organized to elicit them at five levels: doing, echoing, responding, testing, and structuring.

The first three response forms require children to react to a question or directive; the last two require them to use their own initiative. Doing involves a nonverbal response to a question or directive; it indicates comprehension and serves as a fully communicative function. Echoing, which requires children to repeat what has been said, is used when a new word or concept is introduced; essentially this provides them with the correct words to use when responding to a question on newly learned material or concepts. Responding requires that they use their own words to produce a verbal answer to the question, a more difficult language task than either doing or echoing.

Having acquired new information, words, or ideas, children are put into a situation where they must test their grasp of this newly learned material. Now it is their turn to ask questions and confirm or reject the responses received, thereby examining what they know and fitting it into the framework of their previous knowledge.

The most advanced level of language response expected of HIPPY children is for them to structure information or tasks for another to learn and do. In this situation they become the instructors, structuring the situation, activating the other person, and correcting that person's responses. Children who can do this can be said to have mastered the material learned.

Vygotsky (1962) relates language to meaning and meaning to concepts. He suggests that the concept—the highest level of generalization of meaning—is the basis of language as a means of communication. A child may use the word *book* to refer to the book or books in front of him, but until he or she grasps the concept "book" might not use the word in the generally accepted sense.

Language is also a tool for dealing with problems. Changes in levels of the use of verbalization and verbal mediation in young children are associated with the increased ability to acquire new concepts and to deal with new problems (Elkind et al. 1967; Kendler 1963; Lombard 1968; Luria 1961). Young children use language in their daily activities and play to work on new concepts and to overcome difficulties that crop up in the course of play. Luria (1961) presented strong evidence that, without language, children are handicapped in dealing with problems, even play problems.

Since the acquisition of concepts is closely related to the acquisition of language, children's concepts will be limited to the extent that their language is restricted. In the natural home situation, the mother's speech to her children constantly shapes and reshapes their perceptions of the environment. She names objects and relates objects, feelings, and situations that are familiar to the child and encourages experimentation with this new information. She teaches her children what does and does not fit into the concept learned. Both of these kinds of information are important to children's comprehension of the meaning of the words and to their formation of the relevant concepts (Carroll 1964).

Mothers in HIPPY were not expected to be aware that they played a critical role in this aspect of their child's development. Thus in order to increase their sensitivity to the subject and to provide opportunities for children to work on familiar as well as new concepts in a variety of home situations, the HIPPY activities were programmed to include a series of concepts to be worked on through the years.

The concepts that are emphasized throughout the program fall into three general categories: attributes, spatial relationships, and quantities. The first two were prerequisites for advancement in a series of activities for several of the learning games planned. For example, the children had to have a good grasp of the basic concepts of shape and color, and, within each of these concepts, they needed to be able to deal confidently with four different shapes and four different colors. Plastic tiles were used in the typical learning sequence for this type of concept learning (table 3-1 provides an example).

The sequence would be different if everyday concepts of relationships or size were involved. For instance, in activities that focus on the concepts "next to," "between," "above," and "below," mother and child organize and reorganize household items such as pillows, chairs, cups, and pencils in a series of games aimed at enabling the child to imitate, answer, question, and structure. In the last, the child creates the organization of the objects and tests the mother's ability to respond according to the rules he or she

Table 3-1
Typical Learning Sequence with Shape and Color Tiles

Mother Does	Mother Says	Child Does	Child Says	Mother Says
Holds up a green square tile	This shape is a square	Looks and listens		
Holds up a red square tile	This shape is a square	Looks and listens		
	Say "square"		Square	Square
Puts a square and a circle on the table	Show me a square	Points		
Puts out another square and another circle	Show me a square	Points		
Holds up any square	What shape is this?		Square	Square
Puts all the shapes on the table—12 tiles	Find all the squares and pile them one on top of another	Does		
	Find all the circles and pile them on top of another	Does		
	Tell me what you just did		Describes what he or she did	You piled up all the squares and then you piled up all the circles
Points to the piles of squares	What are these?		Squares	Squares
Points to the pile of circles	What are these?		Circles	Circles
Spreads all the pieces on the table	Now you tell me which shapes to pile up		Tells mother to to pile up either circles or squares	
Repeats last action	[Repeats last question]		Tells mother to pile up either circles or squares	

sets out. For example, the child places a book behind and another book next to the standing mother and asks, "Which book is behind you?"

Such household activities are followed by workbook activities in which the child is first asked to identify and choose correctly among pictures of objects or people doing the same kinds of things she or he and the mother did. Finally the child is asked to mark the correctly placed shape, figure, or object in pictures of new situations. When enough concepts have been used in regular activity sequences and there is reason to believe that the child is able to use them confidently, they are organized into lotto-like games, which provide repeated exercise and reminders for both mothers and children.

Activities dealing with the concept of quantity are concentrated in the second year of HIPPY, when all the children are in kindergarten and are working with their teachers on basic math concepts. Here HIPPY activities were planned to be supportive of the classroom curriculum; it was expected that this linking would provide mothers with focuses and skills for activities that would make them feel closer to what their children were doing in school.

Sensory and Perceptual Discrimination Skills: The second broad area of HIPPY activities is that of sensory and perceptual discrimination. The complexity of our world requires that early in life we learn to sort, classify, and discriminate the sights, sounds, and sensations about us in order to enable our further learning. Some of the earliest developmental tasks in children's lives involve activating their senses to gather information about the environment. Lynn (1963) and Piaget (1967) say that it is through repeated interactions with the stimuli around them that children sharpen their perception of the world. Others (Luria 1961; Vygotsky 1962) say that unless the appropriate verbal cues accompany such interaction, learning will hardly be able to take place. Both verbal cues and interaction with the stimuli certainly seem to be needed, as is a strong motivational factor that keeps children at a task and moves them to seek it out and to repeat it time and time again.

Children who grow up in homes where there are toys, space, encouragement, and explanations for their play activities have ample opportunity to acquire perceptual and discrimination skills. Where the early environment does not provide such opportunities, the resultant slower, or even total lack of, development or perceptual and discrimination skills can make children's early years of formal schooling extremely difficult and often fraught with failure (Frostig and Horne 1964; John 1964; Jensen 1962).

About one-third of the HIPPY materials concentrate on providing practice and learning in the field of perceptual and sensory discrimination skills. These are divided roughly into visual, auditory, and tactile skills, in that order of emphasis. There are two kinds of auditory discrimination activities. In the series dealing with pitch and volume, the mother and child experiment with *loud*, *soft*, and *pleasant* sounds on the radio, and they produce *high* and *low* sounds using spoons, glasses, tables, and other household items.

The second series of auditory discrimination activities, which relates directly to language and reading skills, is aimed at sharpening the child's ability to distinguish between similar-sounding words. Rhyming games were devised in which the rhymes included are of the following varieties:

1. Similar final sound, different initial sound (*table-cable*).
2. Similar initial sound, different final sound (*bowl-bone*).
3. Similar final and initial sounds, different middle sound (*kettle-kennel*).

The game forms used are lotto and sound-matching cards. In each case the cue for decision making is verbal and the confirmation or corrective feedback visual (the correct card). Twenty such games are included in the second year of HIPPY.

A variety of "feeling" games are used to develop tactile-discrimination skills. The children identify objects by feel only and are asked to describe them in such terms as *long-short, sharp-blunt, hard-soft, big-little, smooth-rough, round-square, thin-thick*.

Most of the discrimination skills exercised in the program are related to visual discrimination. They are divided into visual-only and visual-motor activities. The first of these activities was designed to give the four year olds a firm mastery over their ability to distinguish between and to use the terms *same* and *different* to describe pictures, as well as to verbalize the basis for their decisions. Several activity series follow in which children match and connect appropriate pictures and symbols, describing what they have done and why. The second series deals with sorting, matching, and describing elements of similarity and difference in everyday items such as coins or silverware.

The visual-motor activities are designed to provide the children with a variety of situations in which they can use pencils, markers, crayons, and the like. Since the mothers in the program expressed reluctance to let their children use pens and pencils for what they called "silly scribbling" before they were able to produce recognizable pictures, figures, or letters, we incorporated the paper-pencil, visual-motor tasks that might have been geared to the free use of writing and drawing tools into tasks that the mothers perceived as serious. Children were asked to follow such instructions as, "Draw the path [predetermined] that the dog must take to get to her kennel"; "Connect the dots and make a picture"; and "Draw a figure like this one [a shape, letter, or number] in all the boxes below.'' The primary objective was to legitimize the child's use of paper and pencil in the home.

"Join the Dots" is a visual-motor activity that occupies a large percentage of the time spent on perceptual tasks during the first two years. Based on the tasks assigned in the fifth subtest of the Frostig Developmental Test of Visual Perception (1961), this series was designed to develop both visual-discrimination and visual-motor skills, as well as problem-solving strategies related to visual-motor tasks. In this series the child is presented with two fields on which nine to sixteen dots are symmetrically placed. A design joins from five to eight of the dots in one field, and the child's task is to replicate this design in the second field. This is a difficult activity for some children, though extremely challenging and fun for most. Mothers whose children find this task difficult are advised to reduce the number of such activities presented at any one time, so that the child may be asked to do only one instead of four, thereby preventing it from becoming an onerous task.

Problem Solving: The program of instruction in problem solving, the third general area of HIPPY activities, was built along the lines of Guilford's model (described in Merrifield et al. 1960). We based our curriculum in this area on the first two of the six factors that Guilford hypothesized as being involved in problem solving: "The ability to think rapidly of several attributes or characteristics of a given object" (p. 6), which includes the ability to list the attributes of objects or ideas, as well as to identify similarities and differences between them, and "the ability to classify objects or ideas" (p. 6), which requires skill in pairing or grouping given objects or ideas. Thus all of the activities relating to discrimination skills, appropriate labeling, and matching and grouping also fall into the category of problem-solving skills.

One of the main problem-solving activities in HIPPY, which runs through the first two years, involves the extensive use of series of matrices. The matrix presents the child with a totally new and different framework in which to solve problems. We adapted Gotkin's model (1968), in which the matrices were intended for use by first-grade children, to four year olds by reducing the initial complexity of the matrices to what can be called a prematrix structure.

The first year of HIPPY activities is used to teach the basic techniques of playing the matrix game, with the matrices growing in size and complexity over the course of the year.

Although the basic structure of a matrix is two-dimensional, to teach the children this structure, the matrices are initially reduced to one dimension:

	Animals	Children
	Dog eating	Boy eating
	Cat eating	Girl eating

A true matrix would be:

	Animals	Children
Eating	Dog	Boy
Sleeping	Cat	Girl

Several weeks into the first year the true matrices—different subjects and different actions—are introduced. The matrices also grow in size from 2 × 2 to 4 × 4 within the first year. To avoid a fixation phenomenon, where the child learns to respond to the given dimensions in only one direction, the same matrix is generally used twice, with the picture order reversed the second time. In the example described above, the second matrix would therefore be:

	Sleeping	Eating
Animals	Cat	Dog
Children	Girl	Boy

The shape and color tiles used in the sensory-discrimination activities are used with the matrices as well. Learning to place all of one color or one shape on pictures that are in a particular dimension eases the child's understanding of the matrix relationship.

In the first year, the content of the pictures deals with subjects and actions restricted to everyday items familiar to the child. At the end of the first year, a card with a question mark on it is introduced to hide any given picture. The child then has to identify the missing picture by using as cues the dimensions relating to its position on the matrix.

In the second year we assume the child knows what the matrix is; it therefore no longer serves as the focus of learning but as a technique to teach and review new content in a game situation. The concepts of size, direction, shape, number, and position, which were taught in the first year, are used as content cues in the second year's matrix framework, as this example shows:

	On Table	Next to Table	Under Table
Toys	Doll	Train	Teddy bear
Books	One book	Two books	Three books
Pots	Large pot	Small pot	Medium pot

In the second year the matrix also becomes a tool to teach children subject matter, such as people at different kinds of work and animals in their different habitats:

	Habitat	*Food*	*Product*
Cow	Barn	Hay	Milk
Chicken	Coop	Grain	Eggs
Sheep	Pen	Grass	Wool

This mode of presentation helps to organize the information for the child and to teach it in categories. Once the child has grasped the idea of how a matrix works, the matrix pictures are presented as individual cards, which he or she can arrange into the appropriate matrices.

The matrix boards, cards, and tiles are used in several kinds of games. The children are asked to designate pictures with the tiles, to locate pictures on a board, to identify pictures missing from their correct place on the board, to use two boards for a lotto game in which the total information (such as books on the table) must be given in order to identify the picture, and, finally, to build their own matrix with a given set of pictures. By the end of the second year in HIPPY, this matrix-building activity involves sixteen cards, some of them containing pictures new to the children.

Because a broad base of skills and concepts is required for problem solving in math, math concepts and activities are included in sixty-five different HIPPY games and activities. These are introduced in the first HIPPY year, with its focus on relational concepts and emphasis on dealing with the concepts of "same" and "different" in identifying, matching, and selecting objects, figures, and groups of both.

The focus of math activities early in the second year is the subject of inequalities. Children first compare sets that vary in number, content, size, and layout. They then advance to matching sets with their corresponding numerals and to dealing with numbers in other contexts, such as drawing by number, reading numbers, and playing number lotto.

In the third year, when the children are in first grade, the HIPPY math activities begin with a review of the numbers 1 through 10 in conjunction with one-to-one correspondence. They are taught to compare sets that are equal in number (2 cups for 2 saucers; 1 cat + 1 rabbit = 1 rabbit + 1 cat) and those equal in number but not necessarily in content or position (3 horizontal lines = 3 vertical lines). Among the games at this stage are counting with the eyes only and counting by twos, threes, and so on.

Simple addition and subtraction tasks are taught by means of activities in which the children are asked to enlarge sets by one or two items, to combine sets, and to separate sets. Activities toward the end of this year deal with time, measurement, and fractions. The children measure household objects, using matches or strips of paper as units of measurement. They play games that deal with the concepts of whole, part, half, and quarter and make clocks to use in time-telling games.

Other activities related to problem solving are seriation, creating sets of pictures of actions or situations that go together or are appropriate for one another, filling in missing elements in pictures of familiar objects, creating pictures from geometric shapes, identifying objects from their outlines, and putting together puzzles made from pictures of familiar objects.

Without the ability to retain what has been learned, there can be no improvement in a child's performance. Therefore activities devoted to the development of memory skills are part of the ongoing HIPPY program. These begin with the youngest children, who are asked to relate from memory increasingly long or detailed sections of stories from books.

In the third year of HIPPY, two series of special memory games are introduced into the program. In the series dealing with visual memory, the children are asked to remember as many things as possible from an array of objects or pictures or to identify what is missing in either case. These activities involve increasing levels of difficulty in number of items presented, the number of items removed, the familiarity of the items, the similarity of the items, and the complexity of the scene. In the series dealing with auditory memory the children reproduce sounds that vary in content, in tempo, and in length.

Program Evolution

The emphasis given each of the three major cognitive areas over the three years of HIPPY activities evolved as preparation of the program progressed. The focus during the first year is on books and on the development of discrimination skills, with only one major series on problem-solving skills. Whereas books are a fundamental component of the program during this year, discrimination skills are considered of major importance in handling the many concept-based tasks prerequisite to problem-solving activities (Merrified et al. 1960).

The second year's program reinforces the first year's work. Because we assume that the children have a basic knowledge of labeling, visual-motor, and discrimination skills, we decrease the emphasis on these and increase the problem-solving activities, including those that teach basic math skills and concepts. The amount of visual-motor activities, considered an important introductory element to later writing, is kept constant in this year.

By the third year, the emphasis shifts, wherever possible, from discrimination skills to problem solving. Thus, a problem-solving element is introduced even into the book-based activities. For example, the children are asked to construct stories from basic information given, and there is an increasing reliance on memory.

Format

Each activity unit in a given subject series takes five to ten minutes, each series being divided into the required number of activity units and programmed over a period of time. Most formal book series comprise eight to ten units, and the discrimination and problem-solving series have as many as twenty-five to thirty. Each day's work comprises one activity from each of two different series and generally takes fifteen to twenty minutes.

The activities are written out in full detail, including the actual words and actions to be used by the mother as well as the response expected from the child and the mother's corrective response. The mothers' guide sheets use pictures as well as texts, the pictures serving as cues to each activity, especially for those mothers whose reading skills are limited, and the text being confined to essential terminology and verbal instructions. These guide sheets for each day's activities are color coded so that the mothers can see which sheets to use on a given day.

The aide, in addition to receiving weekly instructions from her coordinator, is also provided with a detailed description of each activity to help her prepare for her teaching role. Each weekly program packet includes books and materials, as well as the guide sheets, for both mothers and aides and the worksheets for mothers and children. The number and nature of the books and materials varies from week to week according to the activities included.

Child-Appeal Factor

With all our interest in developing a program that would enrich the children, expand their intellectual world, and provide them with tools for school success, foremost in our planning was the fact that our HIPPY clients were to be four-, five- and six-year-old children. The program would not work if the children did not like it. Thus although each task in each activity was first weighed in terms of its value within the framework of the educational objectives, the crucial evaluation determining if it would be included was whether the children were likely to enjoy doing it and would stay with it. The vast majority of the more than nine hundred activities finally selected for inclusion have, in fact, been extremely popular. Those that are not are being revised constantly or completely changed to increase their child-appeal factor.

One of our overriding objectives in programming the HIPPY activities is to show children how much fun it can be to learn. Since this is an integral part of each step of the program, they receive constant reinforcement of the fun as they learn, thereby becoming easier to work with and better able to handle increasingly challenging material. One of the techniques used to teach children that they must resist impulsiveness, keep paying attention, and attend to details is to make frequent changes in the mode of response required—for example, from pointing to marking or from fitting to matching. As their range of response forms grows, their feelings of mastery and pride grow, and their joy in working on the activities increases. The ensuing increase in the mother's satisfaction produces positive interaction, adding yet another dimension to the upward spiral of the enjoyment-involvement-mastery-pride process on both their parts.

Building a Program Designed for Easy Implementation

Although much general research on the education of the disadvantaged went into the structuring of HIPPY, the conclusions drawn from this research would be meaningful only if it could provide the basis for a successful program, one that could be replicated with a high degree of comparability. And the likelihood of replication would be strengthened if that program were feasible in terms of both budget and personnel.

Most adult-oriented programs tend to assume that clients will seek out their service once it becomes known and acquires value for them. On this basis, courses and special activities are offered, discussion groups are organized, and new services are introduced into a community. An examination of the attendance at these adult programs very often reveals two kinds of patterns.

In the first case, attendance numbers are reasonably steady, but there is frequently a large population turnover for every session. This makes an ongoing, progressive program almost impossible, with the likely result that those who do attend the program regularly will find it either repetitive or a series of sessions unrelated to one another. The net result is frequently the cessation of activities and the belief that yet another program has failed to take hold.

In the second attendance pattern, the participants tend to come from the same group, the active core of participants in community programs. Therefore reasonably good attendance at a program of adult-oriented activities frequently belies the fact that only a small percentage of the community's potential participants is involved.

A program that was to involve mothers in the process of enriching their own children had to seek ways of reaching all of the target mothers and keeping them involved on a regular basis, without falling into the usual pitfalls of adult-oriented community programs. Examination of the possible reasons for limited and irregular attendance patterns led us to formulate the hypothesis that mothers do not attend activities outside the home because this requires a great deal of effort and organization on their part.

Since the promise of reward for effort expended is uncertain, the likelihood of getting a mother out at all is slim. And for those who have had such a single experience, the likelihood that it provides sufficient satisfaction for them to want to repeat the effort is also slim. With this in mind and since the original HIPPY model was based on the regular involvement of mothers with their children only in the home, we decided to guarantee the delivery system by having the mothers visited at home at least biweekly. Thus their willingness to become involved in the program would not be completely confounded by their inability to leave the house in order to obtain the weekly activity materials.

Although weekly home visits can be costly in terms of both available personnel and money, the potential for input in home visits is tremendous. In individual home sessions it is possible to adjust the pace of learning to each mother's level of ability, to identify and deal with specific problems as they arise, and to provide mothers with support and guidance as encouragement to continued participation in a new and somewhat demanding undertaking. Our decision to use paraprofessional aides was based on the fact that although highly skilled professionals could establish warm relationships with mothers, guiding them in dealing with their children as well as teaching them how to use the HIPPY materials, the few skilled professionals available for such work were relatively highly paid. In addition, since the HIPPY materials are almost self-explanatory, the need for specially skilled people to deliver and explain them was questionable.

At the time, such use of paraprofessional aides was relatively rare in Israel outside the medical field. Their availability and value had, however, been well demonstrated in the United States with the Head Start programs (Riessman 1966; Karnes et al. 1970b; Micotti 1970). It was expected that what these aides lacked in education and formal training would be compensated for by their ease of access and cultural familiarity. Among the positive side effects expected from paraprofessional staffing of HIPPY was the introduction of local leadership into neighborhoods in which it had been singularly lacking. All those connected with services to these communities were not part of them. The teachers, nurses, doctors, social workers, and their like served the community during working hours; however, since they resided elsewhere, they were not available for guidance and leadership at any other time. The training and work experience of the aides was expected to bring about a rise in their own self-esteem, aspirations, and expectations (Barback and Horton 1970). We believed that by training a group of local mothers to serve other mothers in their own neighborhoods, we could provide these neighborhoods with a much-needed nucleus of active local leaders. In addition, the paraprofessional aides would serve as models for the mothers with whom they worked (Bronfenbrenner 1969; Micotti 1970; Jester 1969). We hoped that they would be able to show this somewhat passive group of women that they too could aspire to change and development in their own lives and in the life of their communities.

The use of paraprofessionals can extend the services provided by professionals, but it cannot replace them fully. A well-trained, highly motivated professional worker was needed to coordinate the local HIPPY activities and to help the aides perform their roles successfully.

There were few guidelines to determine the exact job of the HIPPY local coordinator or the kind of professional best suited to that job. The first HIPPY local coordinator was a master kindergarten teacher who was intensely interested in being part of a new approach to what she had found to be an important issue.

As HIPPY grew and spread to new communities, the program director, who until then had trained all the aides personally, could no longer continue to do so. Therefore the role of the local coordinator, which had originally involved supervision of the aides, was enlarged to include full responsibility for their training as well.

With the introduction of group meetings, the role of the coordinator again had to be expanded considerably. Whereas the aides could be expected to deliver and explain the HIPPY materials to the mothers in their homes, the dynamics of a group requires better-trained and more highly skilled leadership. The local coordinators would therefore be present at the group meetings, taking over from the aides once the materials had been distributed and learned.

When local agencies took over the financial responsibility for the program from the Hebrew University, the local coordinator assumed the role of administrator and liaison between HIPPY and the appropriate community agencies, having to prepare reports, to account for the aides' time and work schedules, to arrange budgets for special events, and to attend meetings of the local committees and public bodies involved.

HIPPY has been relatively easy to administer at the local level. Standards for the aides' salaries are established nationally, thereby making local negotiations unnecessary. Aides are paid on the basis of the number of families in their care. The time they spend in learning their role and the materials to be taught, as well as in preparing for and reporting on home and group contacts, are included in this calculation. They are not, however, paid for time lost when mothers are not at home for the biweekly visit. Although this creates some pressure, it makes for a challenging situation. An aide who gives up on a family loses salary, but if she works hard to help a problem family, she loses time. Although the local coordinator assists in whatever way possible here, the aide makes the final decision. Very few families have been lost from the program due to an aide's unwillingness to pursue them.

Few facilities are needed to implement HIPPY: a safe place to store the large quantities of workbooks and other materials to be distributed, a place in which the local coordinator can keep records and meet with the aides, and places close to where the mothers live for the group meetings. One structure frequently serves all three of these functions.

The materials used in HIPPY are sent directly to the local coordinator according to the number of children enrolled for the year. The materials are supplied centrally in four to six shipments throughout the year. This administrative package has been put into operation by the Research Institute, by municipal departments of education, by local departments of welfare, by community centers, and by local psychological services. The system has worked in every case, apparently because it provides simple, clear-cut guidelines and directives.

The ultimate cost of implementation was a major consideration in the planning of HIPPY. To this end, the written materials and learning aids were designed to be produced inexpensively and the activities to require no additional outlay for equipment on the part of the families. Any model in which individual contact with the participants is the prime mode of delivery is, by its very nature, relatively costly. Although the salaries of the aides are comparatively low, the cost per family of group meetings plus home visits is greater than a standard program with only group meetings would be. Each child in HIPPY costs about one-half the cost of one in a preschool class, and since HIPPY is not suggested as a replacement for preschool, the additional expense is considerable.

On the other hand, remedial teaching for only one year costs 40 percent more than three years of HIPPY. (The costs per child, per year, for each of the three educational settings are: HIPPY, $150; preschool, $310; remedial, $733.) If this, by itself, did not fully justify the cost, the fact that HIPPY is preventative in nature would. The cost of failure to both the child and family must be taken into account although it cannot be calculated in terms of money spent. And when the value of the new insights and patterns of interactions that develop between mothers and their children is added, the cost factor assumes yet new and different proportions. Thus although HIPPY is not an inexpensive program, it gives full value for the outlay involved.

4

The Effect on Children

The research relating to HIPPY has dealt with its effect on all those participating in or affected by the program: target children, mothers and other family members, aides, coordinators, and the community at large. Many of the data collected relate to information gathered from or about the participants at various stages of the program's development. The core of our research data on HIPPY is the result of systematic study and the manipulation of variables that we expected would be affected by the program. Other data reflect the spontaneous reactions of the participants.

HIPPY was based on the hypothesis that home instruction by mothers using specially programmed materials would provide disadvantaged young children with skills and attitudes that would increase their potential for success in school. During the initial research period, this was expanded to include the additional hypothesis that the home instruction administered by mothers would be more beneficial than the same programmed instruction given by preschool teachers in the classroom. An examination of our primary hypothesis would allow us to determine the efficacy of investing in the proposed educational intervention program. And by comparing the effect of the HIPPY materials when administered in the home versus the classroom, we could provide additional information on the efficacy of the mother as special instructor of her child.

Original Tel-Aviv Study, 1969–1972

The original HIPPY study in Tel-Aviv included 161 children in two phases (1969 and 1970). The children were assigned to one of three experimental groupings: home instructed, teacher instructed, or control. All of the children selected were in some type of preschool, all of them came from disadvantaged neighborhoods, and all were forty-seven to fifty-eight months old at the beginning of the study.

Demographic information on the families of these children was gathered prior to their introduction into HIPPY. Their parents ranged in age from eighteen to fifty-seven, most of them falling into the twenty-six to forty-one age group.

Patterns of parent education varied in that more mothers than fathers fell into the low-education group. Eighteen percent of all parents had no

Table 4-1

Country of Origin of Parents, 1969 and 1970

Country	Fathers	Mothers	Total
Israel	15.2%	20.9%	18.1%
Iraq	20.3	22.8	21.6
Iran	24.7	27.8	26.2
Yemen	10.8	4.4	7.6
Syria	7.6	5.7	6.6
Other			
Europe	7.6	5.7	6.6
Asia	13.8	12.7	13.3

formal education; 88 percent of the mothers and 76 percent of the fathers had completed no more than eight grades of elementary school; five fathers had completed high school, with two of them completing two years of college.

Over 75 percent of the parents were born in Asian or African countries. The 18 percent who were born in Israel seemed to be of Afro-Asian background. Only 6.6 percent were born in Europe. (See table 4-1.) Hebrew was spoken in all the homes. It was the only language spoken in 31 percent of the homes and was used along with Arabic in another 29 percent of the homes.

There were two to ten children in each family, all of them living in homes of three rooms or fewer. Seventy-five percent of the families lived in homes of two rooms or fewer.

In the first year of the study the children attended seven different preschool classes. The teachers in two of these classes, totaling forty-two children, volunteered to use the HIPPY materials in the classroom. These two classes were designated teacher instructed. The children in four of the other classes were randomly assigned to the home-instruction or control groups. All of the children in the seventh class were assigned to the control group. Since there was a possibility that some children would drop out of the home-instruction group, a somewhat larger number was assigned to this group ($N = 48$) than to control ($N = 30$).

The median age of the children was fifty-four months. There were about 50 percent more girls than boys, but this proportion was not consistent

Table 4-2

Distribution of Children into Treatments, by Sex and Age, 1969

	Mean Chronological Age in Months	Number of Boys	Number of Girls	Total
Teacher instruction	54.1	13	29	42
Home instruction	53.6	21	27	48
Control	54.6	15	15	30
Total	54.2	49	71	120

across the classes. The teacher-instructed classes comprised twice as many girls as boys, a disproportionate distribution that was unavoidable because the teacher-instructed condition had to apply to all of the children in these classes. Table 4-2 shows the distribution of children by treatment group, age, and sex.

Examination of children in the program for one, two, or three years would yield valuable information on its impact. However, since it was expected that not all the families would complete the three-year HIPPY program, the population was balanced for a valid comparison by adding new five year olds to the sample in the second year of the study. The new children would have only one or two years of instruction.

Changes in Groups

All of the children in the preschools changed teachers at the end of the first year and spread out to a number of different kindergartens. The one teacher-instructed class in the second year comprised seventeen children who had been teacher instructed in the first year and nineteen children not previously included in the study, a total of thirty-six teacher-instructed children. In this year twenty-two new five year olds were added to the home-instruction group, and thirty-six children continued in this treatment group, a total of fifty-eight children in home instruction. The control group had twenty-six children.

The loss of children in each treatment group due to relocation or dropouts recurred in the third year when the children moved up to first grade. The teacher-instructed group was discontinued at this stage because the first-grade curriculum had priority over the HIPPY materials. Since budget considerations required curtailment of the program, we dropped all of the families in the home-instruction group with whom it was difficult for the aide to maintain contact, leaving thirty-seven children in this treatment group. Contact was maintained with all of the children in the control group and with as many of the dropped children as possible, although this became increasingly difficult as families relocated and the children were now spread out over more than twenty-two first-grade classes. Table 4-3 presents a summary of the changes in population sample by year and by treatment. As indicated, the fact that not all of the sample children were available for each testing further reduced the number of children studied.

General Procedure

Three aides made weekly visits to the homes of the children in the home-instruction group, instructing the mothers in the use of the materials and discussing issues that arose from the mother's work with her child. As the

Table 4-3
Instructional Treatments, by Year

	Sample Tested							
	1969		1970		1971		1972	
Home instruction: (HI)								
First wave	48	48	36	35	26	21	No instruction;	
Second wave			22	22	11	10	follow-up only	
Teacher instruction: (TI)								
First wave	42	42	17	15	No instruction;		no instruction;	
Second wave			19	11	follow-up only		follow-up only	
Controls (uninstructed)	30	30	30	26	30	16	30	12
Follow-up								
After 1 yr. HI			12	6	23	12	23	9
After 2 yrs. HI					10	7	21	13
After 3 yrs. HI							26	18
After 1 yr. TI			25	23	28	18	28	18
After 2 yrs. TI					17	12	17	11
Sub-total	120		161		145		145	
Lost permanently or dropped for technical reasons			12		43		49	
Total	120	120	149	138	102	96	96	81

population changed, so did the number of aides, rising to five in the second year and dropping to four in the third year. The coordinator, a master kindergarten teacher, worked closely with the aides during the first two years; she had to withdraw in the third year and was not replaced. Instead the program director intensified her weekly training and guidance of the aides, relying on them to carry out the work in the field on their own. She also visited each family in the program at a time when the aide was instructing the mother.

The teachers who volunteered to use the materials in their classes were helped during the two-year existence of this group by the coordinator who met with them weekly to guide them in the use of the HIPPY materials in the classroom. Most of the classroom activities were structured for small groups, with some of the central activities such as reading a story or introducing a new topic designed for the entire class. The teachers were encouraged to reorganize or leave out any activities or work pages that they found unnecessary or redundant. Although the coordinator helped with this screening, the teachers made the final decision as to what they would use in the class. The coordinator reported that it was generally very difficult to get a teacher either to skip work pages or condense the subjects; although they were prepared to expand on them, they would not do the reverse, expressing a reluctance to "deprive" the children of the activities or work pages.

Once the initial demographic data had been gathered, no contact was made with the parents of children in the teacher-instructed and control groups. The children in the control group had no special program, although some of them were in the same class as were home-instruction children, who sometimes brought the HIPPY material up in the class setting. Although the teachers of the classes that comprised home-instruction and/or control children were aware of HIPPY, they were not involved in it in any way; they were neither shown the materials nor told what they included.

When the children moved up to second grade, there was no further contact with any of them except for testing at the end of that year. Neither was contact maintained with the mothers, although they did meet informally with the aides from time to time to discuss their children's progress in school.

Evaluation

The process of evaluation included assessing the initial equivalence of the experimental groups of children, determining whether the children were in fact learning from the HIPPY materials, and examining the effects of participation in HIPPY on school achievement.

Initial Equivalence: All of the children were tested prior to their assignment to treatment groups. Six tests were used.

The Columbia Test of Mental Maturity and the Goodenough Draw-a-Man Test, which are essentially free from verbal components, were administered in order to establish baseline data on the intelligence of the children.

Sections I and V of the Marianne Frostig Developmental Test of Visual Perception were administered as a measure of the visual perception skills (eye-hand coordination and spatial relations), which we felt were particularly related to the areas of ability that HIPPY focuses on.

A Shapes-and-Colors test was developed to measure the ability to define size (large, small), shape (triangle, square, circle), and color (red, yellow, blue). The children were asked to make these identifications at three decreasing levels of difficulty. A child who successfully completed a task at one level was not required to do the simpler tasks in that section. The three levels of difficulty were verbal labeling, selection in response to a given label, and matching.

A "Same"-"Different" test was designed to measure the ability to use the concepts of same and different by discriminating between pairs of geometric shapes or pictures of objects. The dimensions of difference included content, number, size, and directionality. The test comprised thirty-two paired items; the first sixteen were drawings of commonly known objects such as articles of clothing and household items; the remainder were abstract shapes. Upon seeing each pair of items, the children were to indicate whether they were the same or different.

The data from these tests were analyzed both by class and by treatment group (tables 4-4 and 4-5). In measures of intelligence, the total sample proved generally homogenous. There were no significant differences on the Columbia Test of Mental Maturity, and one of the seven classes performed significantly better ($p < 0.05$) on the Goodenough Draw-a-Man Test. A Newman-Keuls analysis of the difference (Winer 1962) showed that children in this class scored significantly higher than only one of the other seven classes. There were no significant differences on measures of visual-motor functioning (Frostig I and V) or of ability to use the concepts "same"-"different" in a visual discrimination task. An analysis of variance indicated that the children in two classes were significantly better than those in the other classes in their performance on the Shapes-and-Colors test. Since shapes and colors are included in the preschool curriculum for all schools, and pretesting was done in October, probably these two classes received training in shapes and colors during the first six weeks of the school year.

Although the children had been randomly assigned to treatment groups, significant differences in performance were found on three pretest measures. The children assigned to the two experimental instruction groups (home instruction and teacher instruction) performed significantly better ($p < 0.01$) than did their control group counterparts on the "Same"-"Different" and Shapes-and-Colors tests, as well as on the Goodenough Draw-a-Man Test. These differences are probably related to the fact that the children in these two treatment groups were drawn from classes in which performance on these measures was higher. There were no differences on the Frostig subtests or on the Columbia Test of Mental Maturity.

The overall performance on the pretests indicated that the treatment groups were basically similar. The small differences among these were nevertheless taken into account in subsequent analyses.

After Preschool (1970): The battery of tests given at the end of the first year's study program focused on the assessment of learning. It included the "Same"-"Different" and the Shapes-and-Colors tests in abridged and revised forms, the Frostig V (Spatial Relations), and a Matrix test designed to measure the ability to deal with information in matrix form, a skill taught as part of the program in problem solving.

The Home-Story test was devised to test the level of family involvement based on response to school demands. It was administered only in the four

Table 4-4
Means and Standard Deviations on Pretest Measures, by Class

		1 (N = 27)	2 (N = 28)	3 (N = 13)	4 (N = 10)	5 (N = 18)	6 (N = 15)	7a (N = 12)	Total
Goodenough	M	4.0	3.7	5.7	6.3*	3.0	5.2	2.5	4.2
	SD	3.7	3.9	2.9	3.0	4.0	3.2	1.0	3.6
Columbia Maturity	M	30.1	35.1	29.2	36.9	34.8	34.1	30.8	32.9
	SD	10.1	8.4	11.9	11.6	13.9	11.7	10.1	11.0
Frostig I	M	6.3	6.3	5.2	5.7	5.4	5.4	4.5	5.7
	SD	2.8	2.7	2.8	2.9	2.9	2.9	1.7	2.7
Frostig V	M	0.6	0.3	0.3	0.3	0.3	0.5	0.8	0.4
	SD	0.8	0.5	0.5	0.5	0.5	0.5	0.6	0.6
Shapes and Colors	M	74.6*	55.9	72.9	72.5	63.6	77.1*	53.1	66.6
	SD	22.2	16.2	21.0	25.9	25.4	20.0	17.5	22.3
Same-Different	M	21.4	21.0	21.3	23.5	21.0	21.8	19.6	21.3
	SD	5.3	4.8	4.4	4.9	4.1	5.4	0.9	4.6

Note: All mean figures refer to raw scores.
[a]Scores estimated from posttest data.
*$p < 0.05$

Table 4-5
Means and Standard Deviations on Pretest Measures, by Treatment

		Teacher Instruction (N = 45)	Home Instruction (N = 48)	Control[a] (N = 30)	F Ratio
Goodenough	M	3.6	5.7	2.5	9.1*
	SD	3.8	3.5	1.9	
Columbia	M	32.0	34.6	31.7	0.9
	SD	11.9	10.2	10.7	
Frostig I	M	6.0	5.9	5.1	1.0
	SD	2.8	2.9	2.2	
Frostig V	M	0.5	0.4	0.5	1.0
	SD	0.7	0.5	0.6	
Shapes and Colors	M	70.2	68.8	57.7	3.3*
	SD	23.9	22.7	17.0	
Same-Different	M	21.2	22.1	17.8	7.7*
	SD	4.8	4.9	4.9	

Note: All mean figures refer to raw scores.
[a]Includes twelve children for whom pretest data were estimated from posttests.
*$p < 0.01$.

kindergarten classes with both home-instruction and control children. The teacher gave each child a simplified and illustrated version of a story by Leah Goldberg, together with instructions and a work sheet, and told the children, "Give this to Mother and return it the following day." The printed instructions to the mother requested that she read the story to her child twice and complete a short exercise. The following day the materials were collected in the preschool, an an examiner asked each child eight questions about the story.

Means and standard deviation on all measures for all children by treatment are given in table 4-6. Analyses of variance of the posttest scores by treatment show that the home-instruction group performed signficantly better than the control group on all five measures. On comparing the performance of the home-instruction and the teacher-instructed groups on the four tests given to both (the teacher-instructed group was not given the Home-Story test), we found that the home-instruction group performed significantly better on all four measures.

In order to account for the initial differences between the gorups, we computed prediction scores for each child, based on pretest performance and selected demographic variables and compared them with the child's actual test performance. The following demographic variables were used for

Table 4-6
Means and Standard Deviations on Posttest Measures, by Treatment, 1970

		Teacher Instruction (N = 45)	Home Instruction (N = 48)	Control (N = 30)	F Ratio
Frostig V	M	0.9	2.4**	0.9	12.9
	SD	1.3	1.7	1.5	
Same-Different	M	7.8*	10.0**	6.0	20.4
	SD	2.9	2.2	3.3	
Shapes and Colors	M	72.2*	86.4**	65.5	9.1
	SD	23.6	17.7	22.8	
Matrix	M	11.0	12.8**	10.3	6.7
	SD	3.3	3.4	2.5	
Family Story test score	M	—	2.4**	1.0[a]	25.2
	SD	—	0.9	1.1	

Note: All mean figures refer to raw scores.
[a]$N = 18$.
*$p < 0.05$.
**$p < 0.01$.

this analysis: age, sex, classroom teacher, home-instruction aide, father's country of origin, father's level of education, mother's country of origin, mother's level of education, number of children in family, total number of persons in the home, and number of rooms in the home.

The predicted scores were compared with actual posttest scores, and the resulting residual scores were then submitted to an analysis of variance by treatment. Significant differences in favor of the home-instruction treatment were maintained for four of the ten measures. Analysis showed that the posttest differences on the Shapes-and-Colors and the Frostig I tests were not significant (table 4-7). On both of these tests it was found that pretest scores explained about 25 percent of the variance, accounting for the drop in the significance of posttest differences.

In summarizing the results of testing for this period, we saw that children in both the home-instruction and the teacher-instructed groups were learning new materials, the home-instruction group having a clear lead.

Another source of information on the children's learning was the spontaneous reports from their preschool teachers. Although there was much overlap in the teachers' reports, they said that generally the HIPPY children were different from groups of children they had previously taught. For instance, in a mixed class of four and five year olds, the four-year-old children who were part of the program showed greater alertness and responsiveness. On comparing the non-HIPPY five year olds with the four-year-old group, this teacher said that the younger children were more adept in the use of didactic play materials and in small-group activity and appeared to be more alert and responsive to their environment. They frequently called out answers before the teacher finished phrasing the questions. "I find it difficult to work with the kindergartners on the regular curriculum when the four year olds are around, since the latter generally hover around the work tables and give the answers before I have a chance to give the kindergarten children full instruction," said one teacher. She added, "This is a new phenomenon. In [my] previous classes . . . the four year olds tended to ignore the older children during 'lesson time'."

Another teacher reported that the HIPPY children participated more actively during story time and discussions. In the group discussions little probing was necessary, and simple hints were generally enough to evoke a flow of responses and explanations.

Several teachers said that the HIPPY children used more concepts and shapes in their daily activities, including drawing. Yossi, one of the less alert and responsive children, announced when sitting alone drawing shapes: "Now I'm drawing a standing line, and this is a lying down line. I already have a diagonal; soon I'll have another diagonal. I'm making them like a roof."

In general, the HIPPY children were reported to be superior in their grasp and execution of tasks that required use of didactic materials, equaling the five-year-old children in their grasp of the problems involved in

Table 4-7
Means and Standard Deviations on Residuals, by Treatment

		Teacher Instruction (N = 45)	Home Instruction (N = 48)	Control (N = 30)	F Ratio
Frostig V	M	−0.17	0.35	−0.31	3.1760*
	SD	1.12	1.20	1.54	
Same-Different	M	−0.19	0.90	−1.15	7.2518**
	SD	2.39	2.14	2.57	
Shapes and Colors	M	1.90	1.44	0.55	0.6908
	SD	14.11	13.39	14.83	
Matrix	M	−0.46	0.83	−0.63	3.8076*
	SD	2.70	2.64	2.67	
Family Story	M	n.g.	0.55	−0.29	12.3455**
test score	SD		0.84	0.94	

Note: n.g. = Test not given.
*$p < 0.05$.
**$p < 0.01$.

puzzles and learning games (matching, sorting, seriation). One teacher said that she only had to demonstrate a task and the HIPPY children carried on with almost no further guidance.

After Kindergarten (1971): The children in the study were tested again after they had completed their year in kindergarten. This time the tests related to school achievement; the Frostig V measure, the Minkovich Test of Math Readiness, and the Boehm Test of Basic Concepts were used.

The Minkovich Test of Math Readiness is an individually administered test of basic concepts and relationships in math. Developed and standardized in Israel, its purpose is to identify the child's strengths and weaknesses at the beginning of the first grade. It is made up of six sections: counting, sets and fractions, ordinal numbers, one-to-one matching, conservation of quantity, and arithmetic problems. A total score reflects the sum of the weighted subscores.

The home-instruction group scored highest on four of the six subtests and on the total score (table 4-8), although an analysis of variance on these scores showed that the differences were not statistically significant. A sign test performed on the medians, however, indicated that the home-

Table 4-8
Means and Standard Deviations on Minkovich Test of Math Readiness, by Treatment, 1971

		Home Instruction (N = 52)	Teacher Instruction (N = 25)	Control (N = 26)	F Ratio
Counting	M	53.6	50.8	52.3	0.40
	SD	13.3	14.8	10.8	
Sets and	M	48.5	46.2	49.0	0.49
fractions	SD	12.0	9.0	11.2	
Ordinal	M	49.3	47.8	48.1	0.19
numbers	SD	11.9	10.3	11.3	1.91
One-to-one	M	51.4	45.2	50.2	1.91
matching	SD	13.4	13.0	13.4	
Conservation	M	49.2	46.4	45.4	1.65
of quantity	SD	10.5	9.4	8.0	
Arithmetic	M	45.9	42.8	45.9	0.66
problems	SD	12.3	11.3	11.5	
Total	M	51.5	46.2	48.3	1.40
	SD	13.9	14.5	13.1	

instruction group was significantly superior on three of the six subtests (sets and fractions, matching, conservation of quantity; $p < 0.01$) and on the total score ($p < 0.02$).

The Boehm Test of Basic Concepts is designed to measure mastery of the concepts necessary for achievement in the first year of school (Boehm 1967). These concepts can be grouped into four context categories or summed for a total score; they are space, quantity, time, and miscellaneous. The test was administered to groups of two to three children at a time, in a room outside their classroom. Subtest and total scores computed for all treatment groups show that the home-instruction group performed significantly better ($p < 0.05$) on the quantity items. Although their performance on all other parts of the test was also high, a sign test performed on the medians showed statistical significance for space ($p < 0.001$), quantity ($p < 0.001$), and total ($p < 0.001$).

The Frostig V Test (Spatial Relations), which was administered for the third time, once again yielded highly significant differences among treatment groups (table 4-10). A Newman-Keuls analysis on the difference between the means indicated that both the home-instruction and the teacher-instructed groups performed significantly better than did the control group ($p < 0.01$) and that the home-instruction group performed significantly better than did the teacher-instructed group ($p < 0.05$).

The poor performance of the teacher-instructed group can be explained only by the fact that the teachers eliminated much of their regular teaching

Table 4-9
Means and Standard Deviation on Boehm Test of Basic Concepts, by Treatment, 1971

Concept Tested		Home Instruction (N = 57)	Teacher Instruction (N = 25)	Control (N = 26)	F Ratio
Space	M	17.6	16.2	17.3	1.56
	SD	3.5	3.5	3.2	
Quantity	M	12.7	10.9	12.1	3.08*
	SD	3.0	2.9	3.3	
Time	M	2.5	2.4	2.5	0.14
	SD	1.3	1.1	1.0	
Miscellaneous	M	2.1	1.6	2.2	1.69
	SD	1.2	1.2	1.4	
Total	M	35.1	31.1	34.3	2.40
	SD	7.6	7.4	7.7	

*$p < 0.05$.

in their efforts to cope with the HIPPY materials. Even so, they were unable to complete more than 60 percent of the year's HIPPY activities in any one year because the HIPPY materials are designed for individualized instruction. Therefore these children did not benefit from all of the new activity materials, nor were they being provided with the usual curricular experiences that the control children were having in their classrooms.

Thus, at the end of the second year of the study we found that the effects of home instruction, though generally small, were clear and persistent. This overall effect was put to the test as the children entered school in the following year.

After First Grade (1972): In the third HIPPY year all but one of the children were in the first grade (one minimally brain-damaged child was held back for a year of special education). Most of the children were in neighborhood schools; a few had been sent to special religious schools well outside the neighborhood.

Since one of the objectives of HIPPY was to enable the children to be better pupils, we were interested in knowing how these youngsters adjusted to school. The teachers of those who remained in neighborhood schools were interviewed at the end of the first quarter of the year. From their answers to the questions it was possible to rate the children in six areas: academic achievement, enthusiasm, persistence, sociability, initiative, and discipline.

All of the interviews were conducted by an experienced nonstaff worker who had no knowledge of the child's previous or current status within the program. During the interview, however, it became clear that the teachers themselves knew which children were or had been involved in the program. This information had evidently been volunteered by both parents and children.

For the ninety-six children rated, it was found that those in the home-instruction group excelled in academic achievement, enthusiasm, and persistence. There were no significant differences among groups in sociability, initiative, or discipline (table 4-11).

Table 4-10
Raw Scores on Frostig V, by Treatment, 1971

	Home Instruction (N = 57)	Teacher Instruction (N = 25)	Control (N = 26)	F Ratio
M	4.3	3.3	1.7	18.01*
SD	1.9	1.9	1.8	

*$p < 0.01$.

Table 4-11
Significance of Sign Tests on Medians for Teacher Interviews, 1972

Academic achievement	Home instruction significantly higher ($p < 0.01$)
Enthusiasm	Home instruction significantly higher ($p < 0.01$)
Persistence	Home instruction significantly higher ($p < 0.05$)
Sociability	No significant difference
Initiative	No significant difference
Discipline	No significant difference

Evaluation at the end of the first grade was based on three measures: the full Frostig Test of Visual Perception (given for the first time), the Milcan, an Israeli intelligence test for grades one to four, and report-card evaluations to assess school achievement.

The Frostig Test includes five sections relating to various areas of visual-perception performance: eye-motor coordination, figure-ground, constancy of shape, position in space, and spatial relations; the last section was being given for the fourth time. The full test was administered to groups of twelve to fifteen children in their classrooms. Scores for each section were computed, as was a perceptual quotient for each child (table 4-12). A comparison of treatment groups showed that the home-instruction group excelled on all sections, reaching a level of statistical significance on all but eye-motor coordination.

The Milcan is a group-administered test with three subtests: word recognition, seriation, and symbols. It includes norms by both class level and age for ages 5.8 to 10.00 years. The test was administered to groups of twelve to fifteen children in their classrooms during the final months of the school year.

Subtest and total IQ scores were computed for all children by treatment group (table 4-13). Each group included all the children who had ever been in that treatment group and who might at the time of testing be considered in the follow-up group of table 4-3. An analysis of variance of the Milcan scores indicated that the home-instruction children excelled on all three subtests and were significantly higher on the total IQ score ($p < 0.05$).

We recorded the teachers' end-of-the-year assessments provided on report cards as being indicative of school achievement at that time. Scoring systems varied from school to school, but it was possible to equate them, giving scores of high = 1, medium = 2, and low = 3. In a comparison of children who had had two years or more of HIPPY home instruction with those who had no home instruction (including the teacher-instructed group), we found that the home-instruction group scored consistently higher in the three basic subjects of reading, writing, and arithmetic (table 4-14). In arithmetic, the difference among groups was significant ($p < 0.05$).

Table 4-12
Means and Standard Deviations on Frostig I, by Treatment, 1972

Subtest		Home Instruction (N = 38)	Teacher Instruction (N = 29)	Control (N = 16)	F Ratio
Eye-motor	M	16.31	15.90	14.93	0.77
coordination	SD	2.62	4.41	4.27	
Figure-	M	15.55	15.60	12.47	3.15*
ground	SD	4.14	3.95	3.98	
Constancy	M	7.69	6.70	6.33	6.22***
of shape	SD	4.36	3.43	3.77	
Position	M	6.41	5.50	4.87	8.21**
in space	SD	1.24	0.97	1.36	
Spatial	M	6.04	5.00	4.40	5.26**
relations	SD	1.26	2.00	1.96	
Perceptual	M	98.41	91.70	84.73	4.74**
quotient	SD	13.17	15.97	14.63	

Note: Comparison of treatment groups after two years of instruction.
   $*p < 0.06$.
  $**p < 0.05$.
 $***p < 0.01$.

After Second Grade (1973): No contact was made with the children in any of the treatment groups while they were in the second grade; however, at the end of the year (June 1973), achievement tests were administered to those neighborhood classes that had been part of the previous year's evaluation. Seventy-two of the ninety-six children tested at the end of the first grade were available for testing.

Two tests were used for this evaluation: the Ortar-ben-Shachar Standardized Reading Comprehension Test for the second grade (*Mivchan Havanat Hanikra*) and the Minkowitz Math Achievement Test for the second grade. The latter had been developed at the Hebrew University several years earlier for used with disadvantaged children in Israel but had not yet been standardized.

A comparison of the scores of children who had home instruction for two or more years with all children who had no home instruction (including the teacher-instructed group) indicated differences significant at the 0.03 level for reading and at the 0.02 level for math achievement (table 4-15). The test performance of children who had been in the program one year or less was poorer than that of all other groups (Lombard 1973).

Table 4-13
Milcan: Comparison of All Scores, by Treatment, 1972

		Home Instruction (N = 37)	Teacher Instruction (N = 29)	Control (N = 16)	F Ratio
Vocabulary	M	8.244	7.519	7.667	1.40
	SD	2.080	1.784	1.447	
Signs	M	9.733	8.741	9.600	1.17
	SD	2.791	2.332	2.995	
Seriation	M	9.867	8.519	9.000	2.87
	SD	2.332	2.293	2.619	
IQ	M	93.622	86.704	90.200	3.45*
	SD	11.146	11.152	9.451	

*$p < 0.05$.

Table 4-14
Grades on Report Cards at End of First Grade, 1972

Subject		Home Instruction Two and Three Years (N = 37)	No Home Instruction (N = 45)	F Ratio
Reading	M	1.41	1.58	1.61
	SD	0.55	0.66	
Writing	M	1.47	1.70	2.94
	SD	0.56	0.60	
Arithmetic	M	1.41	1.71	4.72*
	SD	0.55	0.70	

*$p < 0.05$.

Table 4-15
Math and Reading Scores at End of Second Grade, 1973

		Home Instruction (N = 31)	No Home Instruction (N = 41)	F Ratio
Reading	M	83.55	75.00	4.64*
	SD	14.62	18.06	
Math	M	83.32	66.15	5.74**
	SD	30.84	29.57	

*$p < 0.03$.
**$p < 0.02$.

Jerusalem Replication Study, 1971-1975

The Tel-Aviv HIPPY study was well underway when we decided to start a second study in another city. We hoped that the new program would enable us to gather information on questions that could not be answered from one study alone or that were not germane to the study as structured in Tel-Aviv. For example, we wanted to learn more about the aide's effect on the mothers and their children and whether the program has a spillover effect on younger siblings.

Population

The Jerusalem HIPPY study was initiated in the fall of 1971 with children in four preschool classes in two disadvantaged Jerusalem neighborhoods. The families of one-third of the children in each class were interviewed, and data relating to family size and parents' origin and education were gathered. Using these factors as predictors of level of school success, the preschool classes were matched; two were selected for home instruction, and the other two were assigned to the control group. All of the 137 children in the four classes were included in the sample, except for four who had moved out of the neighborhood by the time the program of activities began and another three who proved to be untestable.

The children in the Jerusalem sample were somewhat younger than those in the Tel-Aviv study (table 4-16). The parents were older (table 4-17) and the average family somewhat larger (5.2 in Jerusalem versus 4.0 in Tel-Aviv). Living accommodations were approximately the same.

Design

The primary research objective of the Jerusalem study was to replicate the Tel-Aviv study. A secondary objective was to examine the effect of modeling

Table 4-16
Age, Sex, and Previous Nursery School Experience of Children in Jerusalem Study, by Treatment

		Home Instruction	No Home Instruction
Age (in months)	Range	36-58	37-60
	Mean	47	48.5
Sex	Boys	33	40
	Girls	28	23
Nursery school experience	Yes	30	25
	No	31	38

Table 4-17
Age, Education, and Country of Origin of Parents in Jerusalem Study, 1971

	Mothers	Fathers
Age		
18-24	8.7%	4.4%
25-32	42.6	21.9
33-40	40.9	44.7
41-57	7.8	29.0
Education		
None	26.6	17.7
0-8	56.5	62.1
More than 8	16.9	20.2
Country of origin		
Israel	21.2	20.0
Asia	40.7	45.5
North Africa	35.4	32.7
Europe and North America	2.7	1.8

on the aide's work with the mothers and, by implication, on the mother's work with her child. Our experience in Tel-Aviv led us to believe that the home-instruction situation was greatly improved when aides made their weekly visit during the afternoon hours when the target child was at home rather than during the morning when she or he was in preschool. When the child was at home, the aide could serve as a teaching model for the mother, a condition that did not occur when the child was in preschool and modeling could not take place. We were not able to examine the effect of modeling on our Tel-Aviv population because it was confounded by other factors. In Tel-Aviv, home instruction by aides was given in the mornings only to those mothers who did not work, and were literate enough to use the materials without the help of an older child. The Jerusalem study was designed to allow an examination of the effects of modeling. All home visits by the aide were made in the afternoon, but only half the children were involved in the mother-aide instruction hour, enabling the aide to model the desired teaching behavior for the mother. In that part of the sample where the child was excluded from the instruction, the child was to be ignored if he or she happened to be home.

A short time after the program began in Jerusalem, we found several difficulties in our design. It became apparent that women from the population in question found it very difficult to work as aides in the afternoon when their own children were home from school. We therefore had problems in finding four aides who could work the hours required and who met our standards.

Of greater importance to the study was another finding, which emerged within the first few months: the aides had great difficulty ignoring the children excluded from the modeling condition in those homes where model teaching was not to be done. Although the importance of their adhering to the constraints of the design was impressed on them and they were encouraged to discuss this issue during training sessions, they had little idea of how to play a role outside their normal pattern of behavior. Therefore we had little confidence that this aspect of the design was being maintained properly.

A third problem that arose was the age of the children. Since only one-third of the sample children had been visited before being assigned to treatment groups and since we were not aware that the preschools with which we were connected were part of a new Ministry of Education program to lower the age for admission to preschool for disadvantaged children, we found that approximately 25 percent of the sample children were less than forty-five months old. These younger children responded with difficulty to the home-activity materials: it was hard for the mothers to get them interested, their attention span was very short, and many of them could not do the tasks. The whole HIPPY experience was therefore unpleasant for both mother and child. Since this was a new factor and we were not sure how it would develop, we were reluctant at that point to drop these children from the sample. Instead, the mothers were given guidance in how to ease their children's way and were told to reduce the number of activities for each week where necessary and for as long as necessary.

Evaluation

After Preschool (1972): These design problems were reflected in the test results at the end of the first year. In June 1972, the children were to have been over fifty-four months old; however, since we were aware of the fact that some of them were younger and that there had been problems with these children, the results of the tests designed to assess their learning during the year were submitted to a two-way analysis of variance (treatment by age).

The four tests used were section V of the Frostig Test (spatial relations), the Shapes-and-Colors test, the Matrix test, and tests of family involvement. In a two-way analysis of the effects of treatment and age on performance on the four tests, the main effect noted was that of age (table 4-18).

Family involvement was tested twice during the first year: early in the year and again in June. In the first test, the mothers were requested to play a cork-in-the-water game with their children and to complete a worksheet afterward. In this game mother and child watched what happened when

Table 4-18
Effects of Treatment and Age on All Jerusalem Posttest Measures, June 1972

Tests		Ages of Home Instruction Children				Ages of Control Children				F Ratio		
		42-48 (N = 8)	49-54 (N = 6)	55-60 (N = 19)	60+ (N = 21)	42-48 (N = 8)	49-54 (N = 11)	55-60 (N = 13)	60+ (N = 17)	CA	T	Interaction
Home involvement Game	M	1.38	1.17	1.58	1.48	1.25	1.27	1.32	1.41	0.89	1.96	0.55
	SD	0.52	0.41	0.51	0.51	0.46	0.47	0.48	0.51			
Story	M	1.00	1.17	2.11	1.48	1.38	1.18	2.00	1.12	3.83**	0.71	0.43
	SD	1.31	0.98	1.05	1.17	1.19	0.98	1.08	1.11			
Shapes and Colors	M	15.25	14.83	17.26	16.57	14.63	14.27	17.00	16.18	6.52***	2.62	0.03
	SD	2.25	2.32	1.05	1.78	2.45	3.69	1.41	2.79			
Matrix	M	21.38	30.83	36.90	35.71	20.63	26.18	34.62	30.00	8.14***	5.32*	0.30
	SD	8.10	10.27	12.09	12.35	5.48	7.43	9.11	9.32			
Frostig V	M	2.13	2.33	3.00	2.57	0.50	0.36	0.62	0.53	0.65	5.56***	0.26
	SD	1.55	2.16	1.80	1.86	0.76	0.51	0.96	0.87			

Note: Ages are given in months. CA = Chronological Age; T = Treatment.
*$p < 0.02$.
**$p < 0.01$.
***$p < 0.001$.

they put a cork, a bottle cap, a small piece of bread, and a sheet of paper into a bucket of water. On the worksheets they indicated which objects floated and which had not. The second test was the same as that used in the Tel-Aviv study, where the children and their mothers were given a simple illustrated story by Leah Goldberg and a worksheet to read and fill out. Although we expected the results to be higher for the home-instruction group, there were no treatment differences between this and the control group. The two-way analysis of variance did show a main effect for age ($p < 0.01$), but there was no interaction effect.

In the home-instruction versus control-group analysis we found a strong effect of treatment for the Frostig V Test ($p < 0.001$) and a smaller but significant effect for the Matrix Test ($p < 0.02$).

There were no apparent effects of teaching by modeling on any tests, if the nonmodeling condition was in effect during the home visits. On the Shapes-and-Colors test there was a significant main effect for age only.

The results of evaluation after the first year led us to drop all those children who were still too young to enter kindergarten the following year, as well as to return to the original HIPPY pattern of morning and afternoon visits, depending upon which was more convenient for mothers and aides. Sixteen of the home-instruction and twenty-one of the control children were dropped because of age. Another eleven moved away and five dropped out, leaving a total of seventy-seven children (thirty-seven home instruction and forty control) in the Jerusalem replication study sample.

We knew that the loss of over one-third of our population would limit our ability to report on the impact of HIPPY on the Jerusalem children, and we had to delete the modeling versus nonmodeling condition. Nevertheless we decided to continue with the study in order to ascertain whether the program could be replicated.

After Kindergarten (1973): After the first experimental year in Jerusalem, the design of the home-instruction program there followed the one used in Tel Aviv. As in Tel-Aviv, there were no group meetings during this year. In June 1973, at the end of the second year of HIPPY, the children were completing kindergarten. At this time the Frostig V, the Boehm Test of Basic Concepts, and the Minkovich Test of Math Readiness, the same tests as used in Tel-Aviv, were administered to all children in Jerusalem sample.

The HIPPY Children performed significantly better than the control group on the Frostig V but not on the Minkovich Math Readiness Test. Results of the Boehm Test of Basic Concepts showed that the HIPPY children performed significantly better than their control counterparts on the total test and on two of the subtests (table 4-19).

Table 4-19
Means and Standard Deviations on Posttest Measures, by Treatment,
Jerusalem, 1973

		Home Instruction (N = 31)	No Home Instruction (N = 34)	F Ratio
Frostig V	M	3.94	1.62	28.90**
	SD	1.71	1.76	
Minkovich				
Counting	M	51.94	50.00	0.46
	SD	12.09	10.94	
Sets and	M	50.32	48.68	0.38
fractions	SD	10.40	11.10	
One-to-one	M	44.36	49.71	4.62*
matching	SD	10.06	10.00	
Conservation	M	49.36	46.77	0.97
of quantity	SD	11.38	9.76	
Arithmetic	M	43.55	45.15	0.30
problems	SD	11.56	11.84	
Total	M	50.00	48.68	0.18
	SD	12.78	12.14	
Boehm				
Space	M	17.77	16.03	4.60*
	SD	3.12	3.42	
Quantity	M	13.03	11.88	2.83
	SD	2.82	2.68	
Miscellaneous	M	2.61	1.94	4.14*
	SD	1.17	1.46	
Time	M	2.16	2.06	0.17
	SD	1.04	0.98	
Total	M	35.58	31.91	4.79*
	SD	6.78	6.72	

*$p < 0.05$.
**$p < 0.01$.

After First Grade (1974): Results of the Minkovich Math and the Ortar-ben-Shachar Standardized Reading Comprehension Tests administered at the end of first grade showed that the HIPPY children performed better than the control group on reading and that the control-group children were better in math, but in neither case were the differences significant. Teacher assessments at the end of the first grade did not coincide with the test results (table 4-20). The teachers found the HIPPY children to be less adept than the control group on both reading and math.

Table 4-20
Report Card Grades at End of First and Second Grades, Jerusalem, 1974-1975

		Home Instruction	No Home Instruction	t
Grade 1				
Reading	N	21	28	
	M	1.42	1.39	0.20
	SD	0.68	0.57	
Writing	N	20	27	
	M	1.45	1.44	0.03
	SD	0.76	0.58	
Expression	N	16	14	
	M	1.68	1.70	−0.10
	SD	0.70	0.58	
Math	N	21	28	
	M	1.66	1.57	0.49
	SD	0.73	0.63	
Science[a]				
Grade 2				
Reading	N	23	28	
	M	1.30	1.71	−2.25*
	SD	0.56	0.71	
Writing	N	23	28	
	M	1.47	1.92	−2.53*
	SD	0.59	0.66	
Expression	N	18	23	
	M	1.55	1.86	−1.36
	SD	0.62	0.82	
Math	N	23	28	
	M	1.56	1.60	−0.22
	SD	0.59	0.74	
Science	N	8	8	
	M	1.37	1.50	−0.39
	SD	0.52	0.76	

[a]Insufficient cases.
*$p < 0.05$.

After Second Grade (1975): The same two tests in math and reading were repeated at the end of second grade, at which time the HIPPY children performed better than the control group in both areas (table 4-21). Teacher assessments at the end of this year again differed from the test results. The teachers found the HIPPY children to be significantly better in reading (and writing) and better, although not to a significant degree, in math, as well as in science and expression.

Table 4-21
Means and Standard Deviations on Posttest Measures, by Treatment,
Jerusalem, 1974–1975

		Home Instruction[a]	No Home Instruction[b]	F Ratio
1974				
Reading	M	69.97	65.52	1.76
	SD	10.12	9.67	
Math	M	62.03	70.24	2.23
	SD	24.41	16.98	
1975				
Reading	M	83.84	79.48	0.97
	SD	18.15	16.87	
Math	M	79.65	68.10	1.05
	SD	46.36	38.36	

[a]For 1974, $N = 30$; for 1975, $N = 32$.
[b]For 1974, $N = 29$; for 1975, $N = 29$.

Comparison of test performance of the Tel-Aviv and Jerusalem samples can only be made for kindergarten and second grade since the Tel-Aviv children were not tested at the end of the first grade. Of the three tests given at the end of kindergarten, the home-instruction children in both Tel-Aviv and Jerusalem performed significantly better than did the control group on the Frostig V. The Tel-Aviv children performed better, although not significantly, on each of the subtests. While the Jerusalem home-instruction children scored higher on only three of the subtests, they did better on the test as a whole.

On the Boehm Test of Basic Concepts, the Jerusalem home-instruction children scored significantly higher on the test as a whole and on two of the subtests. In Tel-Aviv there was a significant difference between the home-instruction and control groups on only one subtest.

On the two tests given in both Jerusalem and Tel-Aviv at the end of the second grade, the home-instruction children scored consistently higher. The differences between home-instruction and control-group scores were significant in Tel-Aviv but not in Jerusalem, possibly indicating that the Jerusalem home-instruction children had not attained the same level of achievement as their Tel-Aviv counterparts. A comparison of the scores themselves, however, indicates that the home-instruction children in both cities were on the same level in reading, although the Jerusalem group was lower in math (table 4-22).

The control-group children in the two cities also performed at different levels. The Jerusalem control group scored consistently higher on both tests

Table 4-22
Comparison of Means and Standard Deviations on Posttest Measures,
by Treatment, for Jerusalem and Tel-Aviv Samples

		Home Instruction		No Home Instruction	
		Jerusalem	Tel Aviv	Jerusalem	Tel Aviv
Reading	M	83.84	83.55	79.48	75.00
	SD	18.15	14.62	16.87	18.00
Math	M	79.65	83.32	68.10	66.15
	SD	46.36	30.84	38.36	29.57

than did the Tel-Aviv control group, possibly indicating that the Jerusalem sample was on a higher level in general than the sample in Tel-Aviv. If this were so, the gains made by the home-instruction children in Jerusalem, although equal to those made by the same group in Tel-Aviv, would be rendered not significant.

The results of the replication study seem to indicate that although home instruction does improve early performance in math and reading, the effects of such instruction were not as strong in Jerusalem as they were in Tel-Aviv.

Effect on Younger Siblings

One of the secondary objectives of the Jerusalem study was to examine the effect of HIPPY on the younger siblings of the home-instruction children there. It had been suggested that a home-based program that strongly involves a mother might affect her behavior to the point where she would change her mode of interaction with all of her children.

We had planned to administer the Israeli standardized version of the Wechsler Preschool and Primary Scale of Intelligence (WPPSI), the only standardized test of intelligence for this age in which we had confidence at the time, to all younger siblings prior to their entering preschool. The testing was to be done prior to entry because Head Start evaluation testing in the United States showed that preschool entry changed the performance of four year olds on standard tests by as much as one standard deviation upward within a period of six to eight weeks.

When it became clear that almost all of the children between the ages of forty-two and forty-eight months in both target neighborhoods were already in preschools, and since there were no reliable tests for examining children under the age of four, we decided not to undertake the study of the effect of home instruction on the younger siblings of our HIPPY children.

Follow-up Studies

Tel-Aviv, 1974–1979

The findings of the Tel-Aviv study were very encouraging in that they clearly indicated that HIPPY had a strong effect one full year after the program of home instruction had ended. They were especially interesting in view of previous findings, which reported that the early gains made through intervention programs tend to vanish soon after the children enter the regular school system (Westinghouse 1969). The unexpectedly large difference between treatment groups in second grade made further follow-up imperative. Toward this end several attempts have been made to gather information on the children as they move through the grades. No time limit has been set for this full follow-up study; the school progress of the original HIPPY children will be monitored for as long as possible. The children were tested at the end of third grade, and teacher assessments were gathered at the end of fifth grade and at the end of the first quarter of the ninth grade.

After Third Grade (1974): When the Ortar-ben-Shachar Reading Comprehension Test was administered to the HIPPY children who were still in the neighborhood at the end of third grade in 1974, the results showed no difference among treatment groups (table 4-23). Although this may have been a true reflection of the school performance of the children, the distribution of test scores called for further examination. Taking all the scores together, we found that thirty-eight (64 percent) of the children scored over ninety and thirty (50 percent) had scores of one hundred (the maximum possible). Thus this test does not provide an effective measure for distinguishing the levels of reading ability for over half of the children.

The Ortar-ben-Shachar Reading Comprehension Test provides norms for each grade according to type of school (disadvantaged or middle class). Since a standard score of seventy is considered the norm for any one scale this would put the home-instruction children above the eighty-third percentile and all other treatment groups above the seventy-third percentile for the disadvantaged in the second grade. The mean of the combined scores for all treatment groups (76.23) was considerably above the norm for the disadvantaged for that year. The mean score for the following year was even higher, above the eighty-fifth percentile for the disadvantaged.

When the scores for the second-grade children were reinterpreted in terms of the scale of norms for middle-class schools, the score for the whole group fell to below the norm at the sixty-fifth percentile. The home-instruction children were exactly at the norm expected for middle-class children (seventieth percentile), while the others were at the sixtieth percentile for middle-class children. It was not possible to make a similar comparison for third-grade test scores because different test forms are used for

Table 4-23
Math and Reading Scores at End of Third Grade, Tel-Aviv, 1974

		Home Instruction (N = 29)	No Home Instruction (N = 30)	F Ratio
Reading	M	87.59	85.33	0.64
	SD	17.76	18.84	
Math	M	84.21	72.00	0.15
	SD	30.74	32.78	

middle-class and disadvantaged pupils in that year (Ortar and Ben-Shachar 1972).

The Minkowitz Test of Math Achievement given at the end of third grade indicated that although the home-instruction children were still ahead of their no-home-instruction counterparts, the differences were not significant (table 4-23).

After Fifth Grade (1976): After our experience in interviewing the teachers of first-grade children showed that they knew which of their pupils had received home instruction using HIPPY, we avoided making such contacts until the end of fifth grade, at which time the teachers were asked to respond to a short questionnaire on the HIPPY children and their control counterparts. By that time there was little probability that the teachers would know who the HIPPY children were.

We were able to locate fifty-nine of the seventy-two children tested at the end of second grade. As expected, their teachers indicated no awareness of HIPPY and cooperated fully in answering the questionnaire. The children's report-card grades were recorded as an additional source of information on their school performance.

The grading system is not standardized in Israel. There are schools in which children are graded numerically (10-1) and others where the grades are evaluative (excellent-fail). In order to integrate all of the grades into a single system, they were first equated. Since this manipulation might have erased some differences in evaluation, the grades were grouped into quartiles. The formulas used for these transformations were:

Numeric Grade	Evaluative Grade	Quartile
10/9	Excellent	First
8	Good	Second
7/6	Fair, almost	Third
5-1	Almost fair, passing, fail	Fourth

Evaluations of the children's achievement levels yielded a consistent trend in which the home-instruction children were rated higher than the no-home-instruction group (table 4-24). There was a greater percentage of HIPPY children than no-home-instruction children in the top half of their classes in all areas except effort.

Questions oriented toward assessment of the children as learners again showed the HIPPY children to be better in four of the six areas rated (see table 4-25). They were more likely to approach new tasks eagerly and to ask for adult help when they needed it, were active learners, and persisted as long as possible in trying to cope with difficult tasks. The HIPPY children were not quite as good about preparing their homework as were the no-home-instruction group, and they used the libraries less.

The differences between the HIPPY children and their counterparts, whether positive or negative, were small, but do indicate the teachers' general view of the children as pupils in their classrooms.

Questions regarding parental involvement with the school indicate that the parents of HIPPY children had fewer contacts than those of the non-HIPPY children (table 4-26). These findings, however, must be viewed in terms of the realities of the school system wherein parents of problematic children tend to have most contact with the school.

Correlations between teacher responses to questions on parent involvement and their assessment of the children lend credence to such a view (table 4-27). There are significant correlations between parents' having been invited to school and children's ratings in math ($p < 0.004$), language ($p < 0.007$), reading ($p < 0.002$), effort ($p < 0.06$), and homework prepara-

Table 4-24

Fifth-Grade Teacher Evaluations, by Treatment in Quartiles, Tel-Aviv, 1976

	First		Second		Third		Fourth	
Subject	N	Percent	N	Percent	N	Percent	N	Percent
Effort								
HI ($N = 30$)	10	33	7	23	7	23	6	20
NHI ($N = 25$)	6	24	11	44	3	12	5	20
Language								
HI ($N = 30$)	8	27	15	50	5	17	2	7
NHI ($N = 25$)	4	16	7	28	11	44	3	12
Reading								
HI ($N = 30$)	10	33	16	53	4	13	0	0
NHI ($N = 26$)	7	27	11	42	5	19	3	12
Math								
HI ($N = 30$)	10	33	9	30	6	20	5	17
NHI ($N = 25$)	4	16	11	44	7	28	3	12

Note: HI = home instruction; NHI = no home instruction.

tion ($p<0.04$). The lower the ratings in these areas, the more times the parents were invited to school. On the other hand, children of parents who came to meetings and showed interest in their child's progress were rated higher on math ($p<0.03$), effort ($p<0.03$), and homework preparation ($p<0.025$).

By 1979 the children in our original sample had transferred to a variety of schools throughout Israel. After a concerted effort, ninety-nine of the children were located, and, when possible, both they and their parents were asked to respond to a short questionnaire.

Table 4-25
Fifth-Grade Teacher Evaluations of Children, by Treatment, Tel-Aviv, 1976

	Always		Frequently		Sometimes		Seldom	
	N	Percent	N	Percent	N	Percent	N	Percent
Prepares lessons								
HI (N = 28)	12	43	7	25	3	8	6	21
NHI (N = 27)	8	30	11	41	5	19	3	11
Uses library								
HI (N = 30)	6	20	6	20	14	47	4	13
NHI (N = 26)	6	23	5	19	9	35	6	23

	Persists Alone		Gives Up Easily		Doesn't Try	
	N	Percent	N	Percent	N	Percent
Copes with difficult tasks						
HI (N = 31)	15	48	11	35	5	16
NHI (N = 27)	11	41	7	26	9	33

	Eager		Reluctant		Rejects	
	N	Percent	N	Percent	N	Percent
Approach to new tasks						
HI (N = 31)	16	52	11	35	4	13
NHI (N = 27)	12	44	11	41	4	15

	Appropriate		Inappropriate		None	
	N	Percent	N	Percent	N	Percent
Asks for adult help if needed						
HI (N = 30)	13	43	6	20	11	37
NHI (N = 26)	10	38	6	23	10	38

	Active		Passive		Disturbs	
	N	Percent	N	Percent	N	Percent
Attitude in class						
HI (N = 31)	17	55	10	32	4	13
NHI (N = 26)	12	46	10	38	4	15

Note: HI = home instruction; NHI = no home instruction.

Table 4-26
Fifth-Grade Teacher Evaluations of Parents, by Treatment, Tel-Aviv, 1976

Parents	Mother N	Percent	Father N	Percent	Both N	Percent	Neither N	Percent
Attend meetings								
HI (N = 20)	9	45	1	5	1	5	9	45
NHI (N = 17)	7	41	3	17	2	12	5	29
Invited to school								
HI (N = 31)	18	58	2	6	4	13	7	23
NHI (N = 27)	18	67	2	7	1	4	6	22
Initiate meetings								
HI (N = 31)	13	42	2	6	0	0	16	52
NHI (N = 27)	12	44	2	7	0	0	13	48
Interest in child								
HI (N = 30)	15	50	3	10	6	20	6	20
NHI (N = 27)	18	67	1	4	5	19	3	11

Note: HI = home instruction; NHI = no home instruction.

All of the children were in school. The majority were ninth graders in junior high schools ($N = 52$) and vocational high schools ($N = 28$). Five children had been held back a grade, and six were in special-education schools. The rest were in a variety of regular residential schools. Distribution of the children in these educational settings is given by treatment in table 4-28.

While HIPPY and no-home-instruction children are evenly represented in junior high schools and vocational high schools, it is clear that more non-HIPPY than HIPPY children have been either held back in grade or placed in special education schools.

In response to the question on their view of themselves as students, 45

Table 4-27
Pearson Correlation Coefficients for Teachers' Views of Parent Involvement and Children's School Performance, Fifth Grade

Parents		Math	Language	Comprehension	Effort	Homework
Come to meetings	r	0.204	0.145	0.143	0.308	0.372
	sig	0.069	0.147	0.149	0.011	0.003
Called to meetings	r	−0.352	−0.332	−0.371	−0.212	−0.242
	sig	0.004	0.007	0.002	0.059	0.037
Initiate meetings	r	−0.113	−0.122	−0.219	−0.006	−0.066
	sig	0.206	0.188	0.053	0.482	0.316
Interested in child	r	0.261	0.084	0.082	0.301	0.268
	sig	0.028	0.272	0.275	0.013	0.025

Table 4-28
Location of Children in School in 1979, by Treatment

School Situation	Home Instruction	No Home Instruction
Junior high school	25	27
Vocational high school	12	16
Special education	2	4
Held back a grade	1	4
Other	5	4
Total	45	55

percent of the home-instruction and 24 percent of the no-home-instruction children said they were good students. Of these, 55 percent of the HIPPY and 50 percent of the non-HIPPY children said that they were better students than others in their class. This sense of achievement only partially reflects their actual school achievement levels.

Once the ninety-nine children were located, their teachers were asked to respond to a shortened version of the 1976 questionnaire. The seventy-eight questionnaires returned provided evaluative data on the school performance at the end of the first quarter. For the sixty-seven children in regular ninth-grade classes, teachers' evaluations indicated that the home-instruction children were performing better than those who had no home instruction. Quartile ratings of these children in each of four areas of school performance are presented in table 4-29.

The eleven children who were in special-education classes or who had been held back in grade represent 14 percent of the seventy-eight children for whom teachers' reports were available. This is about the same percentage reported for the long-term follow-up study of the effects of Head Start (Lazar et al. 1977), where the special-education placements ranged from 11 to 21 percent for the total population studied.

Examination of the distribution of children in these two categories shows a clear advantage for the HIPPY children (table 4-30), one that resembles that found in the long-term study. Lazar et al, suggested that the reduction in the number of children assigned to special education due to their participation in the early-intervention programs can be demonstrated by calculating the difference between the percentage of control and experimental children who were in special education, and then dividing that number by number of children in that population who would have been expected to be in special education, as represented by the control children. Thus, for the HIPPY Tel-Aviv follow-up, the calculation would be a 50 percent reduction in the number of children assigned to special education. Similarly there is a 75 percent reduction in the number of children held back in grade. Reductions in assignment to special education reported by Head

Table 4-29
Ninth-Grade Teacher Evaluations, by Treatment in Quartiles

	Quartiles							
	First		Second		Third		Fourth	
Subject	N	Percent	N	Percent	N	Percent	N	Percent
Effort								
HI (N = 32)	8	25	16	50	6	19	2	6
NHI (N = 22)	8	25	15	47	7	22	2	6
Language								
HI (N = 33)	5	15	14	42	12	36	2	6
NHI (N = 34)	2	6	15	44	15	44	2	6
Reading comprehension								
HI (N = 33)	6	18	15	45	12	36	0	0
NHI (N = 34)	5	15	16	47	10	29	3	9
Math								
HI (N = 33)	4	12	11	33	12	36	6	18
NHI (N = 34)	3	9	10	29	15	44	6	18

Note: HI = home instruction; NHI = no home instruction.

Start follow-up studies range from 50.5 percent to 90 percent, with much smaller changes for retention in grade.

The longitudinal studies of the effects of participation in Head Start have shown that the long-term effects achieved provide full educational and fiscal justification for the continuation of the program. In reporting the results of the fourteen longitudinal studies, Lazar et al. (1977) cite improvement in the children's ability to meet the minimal school requirements and the smaller number of children assigned to special-education classes or held back in grade. Where children began preschool programs at an earlier age and the program had clearly defined goals for parents, with parent involvement and home visits, the children were most likely to succeed in school (Vopava and Royce 1978).

Weikart and Schweinhart (1979) suggest that in addition to clear cognitive gains, the Head Start children are more receptive to the demands of education and adjust better to school. They suggest that, in addition to clear cognitive gains, the total preschool experience produces behaviors in these children that lead others to interact with them "in a manner that provides more opportunity and support which the individual can accept and utilize for growth" (p. 5). Some of the effects of this kind of instruction may be reflected in the "generally positive image of themselves" reported

Table 4-30
Distribution of Children Held Back in Grade or in Special Education, December 1979

	Home Instruction (N = 33)		No Home Instruction (N = 34)	
	N	Percent	N	Percent
Held back in grade	1	3	4	12
Special education	2	6	4	12

by these youths when comparing themselves to their peers in school (Karnes et al. 1978, p. 23).

In comparing the follow-up data on HIPPY and Head Start, it must be remembered that in the Head Start designs reported the children had either classroom or home-based enrichment, or both, while their control counterparts had neither. In the HIPPY design all the children were attending preschools, with the HIPPY children receiving additional home instruction. Thus the comparison between programs goes further than an examination of the effects of intervention because the *HIPPY data yield information on the effects of home instruction in addition to a regular preschool (intervention) program.* Data from the Head Start longitudinal study show that the gains made by children in preschool are both significant and long lasting. The gains made by HIPPY children are even greater than those that would have been made with preschool enrichment alone.

Jerusalem 1976-1977

No achievement tests were given in Jerusalem at the end of the third or fourth grades. Teacher assessments at the end of the third grade showed the HIPPY children to be better, though not significantly so, in math, writing, and science but not in reading. At the end of fourth grade, the HIPPY children were assessed higher in reading, writing, expression, and science, with the greatest difference between the HIPPY children and the control group in reading, although none of the differences was significant (table 4-31).

It was not possible to distribute questionnaires to the teachers when these children were in fifth grade. We expect that in two years, when they enter the ninth grade, data will be gathered similar to that gathered on the original Tel-Aviv study children, and the findings of the two studies will be compared.

Table 4-31
Report Card Grades at End of Third and Fourth Grades, Jerusalem,
1976-1977

		Home Instruction	No Home Instruction	t
Grade 3				
Reading	N	21	21	
	M	1.61	1.57	0.22
	SD	0.81	0.60	
Writing	N	21	21	
	M	1.66	2.04	−0.17
	SD	0.73	0.74	
Expression	N	20	21	
	M	1.90	1.80	0.30
	SD	0.79	0.81	
Math	N	21	21	
	M	1.76	1.80	−0.19
	SD	0.76	0.81	
Science	N	14	18	
	M	1.78	1.94	−0.59
	SD	0.80	0.73	
Grade 4				
Reading	N	19	22	
	M	8.68	8.00	1.82
	SD	0.82	1.44	
Writing	N	19	22	
	M	7.89	7.27	1.63
	SD	1.10	1.30	
Expression	N	19	20	
	M	7.84	7.50	1.03
	SD	0.83	1.23	
Math	N	19	20	
	M	7.31	7.45	−0.33
	SD	1.10	1.53	
Science	N	4	3	
	M	7.89	7.50	0.97
	SD	1.40	1.14	

Implementation Study, 1976-1979

Purpose

When the Ministry of Education adopted HIPPY for national implementation in 1975, its research department requested that the implementation be accompanied by an independent ongoing study of the effects of the program on the participating children. The original research had been undertaken by the program developers. The continued effectiveness of HIPPY, as a fully functioning package, now required reexamination.

A five-year implementation study was initiated in the spring of 1976, carried out by Dr. Yacov Kariv and Paula Silberstein of the Research Institute. Kariv's (1976) chief concern was to replicate the measurements used in the original HIPPY study.

Design and Procedure

The guidelines for the implementation of HIPPY in any one community did not allow for any one segment of the exact target population (for example, the specific preschool classes designated for inclusion) to be excluded for use as a control group. Accordingly Kariv drew the control-group children from adjacent but similar communities that were not included in HIPPY. Because these children represented different neighborhoods and there was a strong possibility that they would ultimately attend different schools, there was a danger that any comparison between the HIPPY and control children would be confounded by the effects of school and neighborhood. Therefore the older siblings of these children, who were in grades one, two, and three, were incorporated into the research design for comparison purposes. This allowed examination of the differences among siblings across as well as among treatment groups and comparison of the performance of the target children with that of the non-HIPPY controls.

The eight communities included in Kariv's sample represented rural, small-urban, and large-urban locations, where HIPPY was just being introduced. A total of 309 families (206 HIPPY and 103 control) were studied. In each family there was one preschool child and at least one other sibling in grades one to three at the beginning of the study. The total number of children studied was 711 (309 preschool and 402 older siblings).

The Siblings

The researchers administered the same standard tests of math and reading achievement used in the original study to the older siblings at the end of the 1976, 1977, and 1978 school years. Only those siblings who had been in first or second grade in 1976 were tested at the end of 1977, and only those who had been in the first grade in 1976 were tested at the end of 1978 (the siblings thus were not tested after they had completed third grade).

The two years of testing and data gathering on the siblings consistently indicated small differences on all measures in favor of the control group, but none of them was significant. This may indicate that there was a difference between the HIPPY and the control groups in the sample and that the HIPPY children represented a weaker group. The researchers suggest that the incorporation of the sibling comparison in the design compensates for any small initial skew.

The math and reading achievement scores in grades one and two showed sex differences: the girls generally performed better in reading and the boys in math.

The greatest variance in sibling scores was attributed to the schools. The school effect for both math and reading was significant for all scores, except for reading in the second grade in the second year of testing. Since both HIPPY and control children are represented in all of the schools, it is suggested that this effect would not be felt in the final analysis.

In summarizing these data, Kariv and Silberstein indicate that test results on the siblings yield information on the equality of the experimental and control groups and on the validity of the measures used. The two groups were found to be unequal, but not to the extent where this would render subsequent analysis problematic. The researchers suggest that the comparisons between sibling groups provide an adequate correction for any inequalities between the HIPPY and control group. The validity of these tests was indicated by the high correlation between the children's math and reading scores over the years ($r < 0.06$, -0.70).

After Kindergarten (1977)

The preschool teachers of the HIPPY children in each of the eight communities were interviewed by the researchers at the end of the first year of the study. The twenty-six teachers interviewed included at least two representatives of each of the eight locations involved in the research design. The teachers selected in each location were those listed as having the largest number of HIPPY children in their classes. Two teachers were dropped from the analysis after the interviewers found that they were teaching for the first year. The data reported therefore reflect interviews with twenty-four teachers.

All of the teachers were interviewed in their free time, either in the classroom or at home. They were asked whether they believed there was a difference between the HIPPY children and children from similar families whom they had taught in previous years. Using a structured form, the interviewer then probed for the teacher's evaluation of the children in specific areas, recording the answers verbatim. The teachers' views on the children's functioning were classified into four general categories: intellectual, motivational, emotional, and environmental, which encompassed twenty-five specific variables:

Intellectual

1. General improvement: Easier to teach, greater development; more alert.
2. Language improvement: Vocabulary; expressiveness; use of longer, more complex sentences; and so forth.
3. General use of concepts.

4. Basic concepts: "Above"-below"; "big"-"little"; "same"-"different; colors; and so forth.
5. Geometric forms.
6. Numbers and quantities.
7. Improvement in work habits, such as concentration and organization.
8 New use of materials: Scraps, sounds, looking through books, and so forth.
9. Educational games, such as puzzles and constructions.
10. Fine-motor coordination, including cutting, pasting, and holding a pencil.
11. Improvement in creative activities: Drawing, use of imagination.

Motivation

12. General improvement: Curiosity, initiative, and the like.
13. Increased motivation in creative activities, such as drawing and coloring.
14. Increased motivation with books.
15. Increased pleasure in familiar things.

Emotional

16. Self-confidence (stands up for rights).
17. Independence in play and in drawing.
18. Improvement in social relationships: Openness, cooperation, sharing experiences, and so forth.
19. Behavior more suitable to preschool in everything relating to discipline and responsibility.
20. Increase in number of approaches to the teacher, which encompasses requests, questions, asking permission, and so forth.

Environment

21. The HIPPY experience as expressed by the children.
22. The HIPPY experience as expressed by the parents (hesitation or enthusiasm).
23. The HIPPY experience as expressed by the preschool teachers.
24. The parents' relationship vis-à-vis the preschool (interest; cooperation; regard)
25. Parents' learning about their children (child growth and development; focus on intellectuality; openness to new techniques; interest in the child; strengthening the bond between parent and child).

For each of the twenty-five dimensions the teachers' responses were graded as indicating that the children were better than (+), not as good as (−), or equal to (0) her pupils in previous years. Variables that the teachers mentioned spontaneously were given greater weight than those that arose only in response to questioning. Variables that were not mentioned at all received no grade. Table 4-32 lists the variables in order of the percentage of kindergarten teachers who mentioned them. (Variables 3 and 4 in the original list have been combined in the final tally under "Concepts").

Two thirds of the teachers reported improvements in their current classes. At least 50 percent mentioned improvement in the areas of concepts, work habits, motivation, and language. From a statistical point of view, those areas mentioned by at least 17 percent of the teachers were significant at the 0.05 level, and those reported by at least 29 percent were significant at the 0.01 level of confidence. Thus twenty-two of the twenty-four variables were within the range of significant differences. The second greatest areas of improvement reported concerned relations between the parents and the preschool. Parents' attitudes to the preschool and their interest in their children were mentioned by over 54 percent of the teachers.

When the responses were analyzed according to the four general categories, it was found that teachers reported changes in general environment (46 percent), in motivation (45 percent), in intellectual functioning (38 percent), and in emotional behavior (28 percent).

Table 4-32
Percentage of Teachers Indicating Change Due to HIPPY

General improvement	67
Parents' relationship to preschool	58
Concepts	58
Work habits improved	54
General motivation	54
Motivation to creativity	54
Parents learn about children	54
Language improvement	50
Talk of HIPPY (children)	50
Pleasure in the familiar	46
Improved social relations	42
Talk of HIPPY (parents)	38
New uses of materials	38
Geometric shapes	33
Self-confidence	33
Independence	33
Educational games	29
Improved creativity	25
Fine-motor coordination	25
Motivation with books	25
Counting and quantities	17
More appropriate behavior	17
Talk of HIPPY (teacher)	13
More approaches to teacher	13

In their discussion of this report (Kariv and Silberstein 1977), the authors suggest that the data be viewed with considerable caution since the teachers may have thought that the interviewer represented the program. If this were the case, their responses may have reflected their desire to please the interviewer as much as their desire to give their personal views on the subject.

To examine the strength of the bias in answering, several different analyses were undertaken. The clearest results came from an examination of the degree of positive responses in relation to the overall reported success of HIPPY in the community. It was expected that were the program not going well, the teachers' reactions would change accordingly.

HIPPY closed down as a result of technical difficulties in two of eight communities included in this study. In a third community the teacher clearly indicated displeasure with the way the progam was being handled. Teachers were found to be divided according to the success of the program in their communities. When their responses across the four general categories (intellectual, emotional, motivation, and environment) were compared, they were found to correlate significantly ($p < 0.02$) with the apparent success of local program. It was suggested that this reinforced the validity of the teacher responses as originally reported.

After First Grade (1978)

The final phase of the Kariv-Silberstein study began in the spring of 1978 when the HIPPY children were finishing first grade. Data available on older siblings included math and reading achievement for grades one to three.

The main objective of the overall study was to determine the effect of HIPPY on the school achievement of the participating children, especially in the early grades. Although achievement tests had not been administered to the original HIPPY populations at the end of the first grade (1971), the scores of the HIPPY children in this study were to be compared with those of their control counterparts and of their own siblings.

Since two of the eight locations chosen for this study withdrew from HIPPY, the sample tested at the end of the first grade in 1978 was now limited to the 223 target children left, evenly divided between the experimental and the control groups.

Difference scores were computed on reading and math performances for seventy pairs of first-grade children and their siblings who had been in first grade three years previously (fifty-two HIPPY and eighteen control). There were significant differences in scores between the HIPPY and control children in both math ($p < 0.003$) and reading $p < 0.045$. These data are presented in table 4-33.

Table 4-33
Difference Scores in Reading and Math, First Grade

		Mean	SD	t	p[a]
Reading	HIPPY	− 2.83	11.28		
	Control	− 11.78	11.19	2.91	0.003
Math	HIPPY	− 6.00	33.01		
	Control	− 21.17	29.31	1.72	0.045

[a]One-tailed.

Further examination of the data reveal several other interesting findings, the most striking of which is the fact that the younger target children in both groups performed less well than their older siblings. The fact that the younger HIPPY children did less poorly than their control counterparts can be taken as an indication that participation in HIPPY was helpful in preventing a still further drop in their performance level.

Comparison of the scores of HIPPY and control children, without reference to their older siblings, reveals no differences between them (table 4-34).

Had Kariv made no provision for including information on the older siblings, there would have been no hint of the data provided by the difference scores. Since the scores for older siblings indicated a definite, though not significant, advantage for the control group, the loss of younger siblings was of greater significance, even though their performance level was equal to that of the HIPPY children.

Kariv and Silberstein (1978b) suggest that siblings included in the comparison group may have been atypical of the siblings in general. They examined this possibility by comparing third-grade math and reading scores for all siblings, by year of examination (table 4-35). Although a main effect was found for year of examination, the fact that the siblings used for the 1978 comparison were the weakest of the three yearly waves indicates that the significance between difference scores of the target children is not due to this factor.

Table 4-34
Raw Scores in Reading and Math, First Grade

		Mean	SD	t	p[a]
Reading	HIPPY	19.2	9.7		
	Control	19.8	17.3	− 0.29	0.61
Math	HIPPY	57.7	23.2		
	Control	56.4	28.2	0.27	0.39

[a]One-tailed.

Table 4-35
Reading and Math Scores for Siblings in Third Grade, by Treatment and Year of Testing

	Reading Mean Score		Math Mean Score	
Test Year	HIPPY	Control	HIPPY	Control
1976	25.3	27.1	76.9	83.9
1977	24.2	21.8	63.6	66.3
1978	21.0	22.0	55.2	61.5

After Second Grade (1979)

Second-grade tests of math and reading achievment were administered to the target children in the spring of 1979. Difference scores were computed for 130 pairs of children and their siblings (73 HIPPY and 57 control). The difference scores of the HIPPY children were smaller than those of the control group but not significantly so (table 4-36).

When family background variables were taken into consideration, the education level of mothers was found to be a contributing factor. Using mother's education as a covariant in the comparison between scores of HIPPY and control children, the analysis indicated significant differences in math achievement scores between HIPPY and control children (table 4-37)

The comparison of children's test performance shows that although the level of the control children in both reading and math improved over the years, the HIPPY children in the implementation study did not achieve the same level of those studied in 1973 (table 4-38). Since we know that the siblings of the HIPPY children tested in 1979 also performed less well than their control counterparts, the difference in the second-grade scores apparently reflects overall differences in performance level between the two groups of HIPPY children. Although HIPPY's impact on this group seems to be smaller, the fact that it does exist is evidenced by their higher math scores and competence equal to that of their siblings in reading.

Table 4-36
Difference Scores in Reading and Math, Second Grade, by Treatment

		Mean	SD	F	p
Reading	HIPPY ($N = 73$)	− 0.863	14.79	0.07	0.78
	Control ($N = 55$)	− 1.491	10.05		
Math	HIPPY ($N = 67$)	− 3.209	46.497	2.07	0.15
	Control ($N = 57$)	− 15.544	48.326		

Table 4-37
Difference Scores in Math in Second Grade, with Mothers' Education as Covariant

	Mean	SD	F	p
HIPPY (N = 61)	– 2.75	47.40	4.05	0.05
Control (N = 54)	– 16.44	47.55		

Because the data on these second-grade children were gathered at the same time as the ninth-grade Tel-Aviv follow-up study was taking place, an effort was made to gather information on the current educational status of the children who had been dropped from the sample over the years. These were classified into two general categories: children who had been dropped due to mobility (change of school or residence) and children who had been dropped for educational reasons (left back a grade or placed in a special-education setting). Follow-up data reported in other studies of the effects of intervention indicated that larger numbers of untreated children had educational problems in grades nine through eleven, but no data had been reported on the effects of intervention on educational status in the lower grades.

In the implementation study, more of the target children than their siblings were dropped from the sample over the years, but for the HIPPY group (both target children and siblings), the reasons were primarily those of mobility, while for the control children the reasons were primarily educational (figure 4-1). Looking at these data from a slightly different perspective, we find that the percentage of children dropped for educational reasons was quite different for the four groups. More siblings (HIPPY and

Table 4-38
Comparison of Second-Grade Scores for Original HIPPY and Implementation-Study Children

			Reading		Math	
			Mean	SD	Mean	SD
HIPPY	1973		83.55	14.62	83.32	30.84
	1979	Target	75.50		81.08	
		(Siblings)	(76.00)		(83.81)	
Control	1973		75.00	18.06	66.15	29.57
	1979	Target	78.00	73.47		
		(Siblings)	(82.50)		(89.13)	

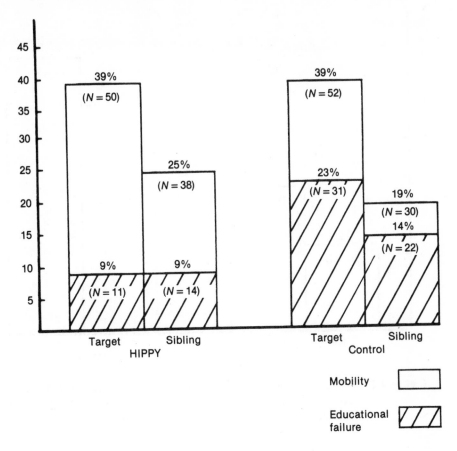

Figure 4-1. Children Dropped from Sample for Reasons of Educational Failure or Mobility, by Age and Treatment

control) and more control children (target and siblings) were dropped for this reason (figure 4-2).

If children in the implementation study can be followed through elementary and junior high school, we will be better able to compare both their achievement levels and their educational status with those of the HIPPY children in the original study as well as with those in Head Start studies. Although the initial data do indicate similar patterns, whether the effects of HIPPY as shown by the implementation study will equal those found to date in the original study can be determined only with time.

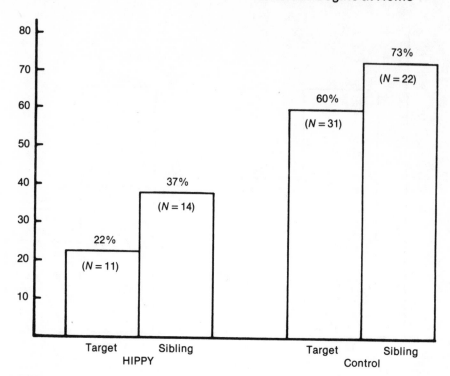

Figure 4-2. Children Dropped for Educational Reasons as Percentage of Total Number of Children Dropped from Sample, by Age and Treatment

5

Participants' Views of the Program

The data presented here on HIPPY's effect on mothers and aides were gathered over the years from children, mothers, aides, coordinators, and teachers connected with HIPPY groups throughout Israel. The data from coordinators were recorded in their monthly or annual reports. Still other data, gathered by graduate students at the Hebrew University School of Education who observed, interviewed, and tested the mothers and aides from time to time, concentrate on the specific areas of interest of each group of students. We have not undertaken a systematic study of the mothers and aides in the program, relying instead on the heavily anecdotal materials reported back to the Research Center.

One serious criticism of soft data is that is it usually drawn from those in a program who are happy in their participation, and it excludes the discontented and those whom the program has failed to help. Although this is generally true, most of the mothers who are not happy with HIPPY, in which participation is strictly voluntary, drop out of the program rather than continue discontented. The number of such dropouts over the years has been between 12 and 16 percent of all participants in any one year, or 22 to 25 percent over three years. The data reported here therefore represent the large majority of mothers who have chosen to complete the program.

Impact on Mothers

One of our early assumptions in planning HIPPY was that the kind of activities it comprises would present a threat to mothers whose own school history may have involved a large degree of failure. In fact, we found that many of the mothers approached were prepared to take the chance that they could cope with the materials. And the low dropout rate indicates that the HIPPY materials have been structured so they were not too threatening for our target mothers.

On the other hand, an examination of the illiterate mothers who were approached to join HIPPY shows that whereas they comprised only about 10 percent of the mothers in a particular community, they represented 25 percent of those who never joined or who withdrew after they tried one week's workbook. In other words, 70 percent of the illiterate mothers did not consider themselves capable of dealing with a program like HIPPY, even when they were offered help with it.

The remaining 30 percent who did join HIPPY used a good deal of ingenuity in finding ways to remember what had to be done in order to teach their children. One typical method was for a mother and her aide to develop a system of signs that the aide marked in the workbook and the mother used to guide her child. Sometimes older siblings were called upon to work with the HIPPY children of these illiterate mothers, and in one case the father, who was literate, assumed responsibility for the story-reading activities.

A different reason for mothers' not joining the program or dropping out early, although it arose much less frequently than the illiteracy factor, was the number of young children in the family. Fifty percent of the mothers approached who did not sign up or who withdrew early had children under the age of two; this compares with 40 percent in the participating families. Although this may not be viewed as the determining factor, when viewed in conjunction with the data on illiteracy it probably indicates that HIPPY is not appropriate for families in which an illiterate mother has several very young children.

The prime cause for dropping out of HIPPY is the general functioning of the family as a unit. Families that are disorganized, under extreme stress, or in crisis have a reduced likelihood of continuing with HIPPY throughout the year. Over the years we have learned to recognize signs that a family is in such a situation, and many local coordinators decide to exclude them from the program in order to prevent their being put into yet another stressful situation with its high potential for failure. Alon (1980) tested mothers' self-concept at different points in their participation in HIPPY. Her tentative findings on mothers who drop out early indicate that they undergo a drop in self-esteem, which lasts two years or more.

Between 1976 and 1978 we requested the local coordinators to gather information on mothers' views of the program. Several coordinators devoted a part of the group meetings to questions such as, "What pleases you most/least about your participation in HIPPY?" and "In what ways has your child changed since you've been working together on the HIPPY materials?" Although the questions were not likely to produce negative responses in the group setting due to politeness and the desire to please, nevertheless we could pick out what was of special interest to the mothers from a selection of the focuses within each response.

The comments reported in this chapter are representative of mothers in ten different communities. In one community the comments were recorded in response to a partially structured questionnaire given by the aides at the end of the year. In another community the comments were culled from the recorded responses to a variety of questions asked by an outside observer who visited mothers in their homes and in the group meetings. The rest are from comments recorded at group meetings and from the aides' weekly reports.

One of our primary assumptions in structuring HIPPY was that it would provide mothers with a feeling of success that would reinforce their participation. If they were to see positive changes in their children's performance level, they would value their part in bringing this about even more highly, feel even more successful, and thereby increase their chances for success even more.

Reports from the field verify both dimensions of this assumption. Mothers do view some of their children's success as their own. One aide reported that "the mother is very satisfied that she can command her child's attention via her work with the program." That mothers also connect changes in their child's attitudes and behavior with success in the program can be seen from the following comments:

> Last year I had to force him to sit and work, but this year he takes the books and works on them by himself—and he also likes to play on his own.

> My daughter didn't understand anything at the beginning. She didn't even grasp what a workbook is or what you do with it. Today she is progressing nicely; even her teacher sees real progress. Today she's begun to understand what is being said to her, and she does things well.

> If I read him a story he immediately shows me the pictures connected with that story. That's progress! When I tell him to bring me a certain book he knows right away which book to bring. He knows the book and what's in it, and that's progress. That's knowledge. It's understanding. It trains him to remember something.

> Now she wants to draw, to work, to be active. She has learned colors and geometric forms, and it was only after starting the program that she began collecting and gluing things. Before she used to do that only in nursery school. I didn't know that she needed to work and draw at home too. Her vocabulary has grown.

The mothers see a rise in their children's level of achievement and talk about it with pride:

> She's more alert than all her brothers because she is absorbed in what she's doing and has benefited from the atmosphere of learning and work.

> Listen, I'll tell you a story. A little while ago we took a trip in our car, and all the way the girl compared the parts of the road—the dividing line, the broken line, the signal lights, the different buildings—to what she saw in the HIPPY pages.

> The program gives a child confidence in math, in drawing, in "same"-"different," in drawing lines, and more. He can get this better from his mother than from someone else. And I also enjoy the child. I have a little knowledge about his education. He only wants me to work on the book with him because I go to work and don't give him that much time, and this is his opportunity.

Working with her child on a regular basis provides a mother with a further sense of pleasure and success:

> I see my child enjoying his work and I enjoy that.

> I spend more time with my child, and this gives me a good feeling and encourages her.

Many mothers report an improvement in the bond between them and their child. One mother of five, speaking about the change in her child since they started working with HIPPY, said that she feels he loves her more and discusses many more subjects with her now. She feels closer to him now as well.

There have been reports that mother-child tensions have been resolved through participation in the program. One mother had a difficult relationship with her four-year-old daughter, who only wanted and paid attention to the father. When HIPPY forced the issue, the child gradually agreed to work together with the mother on the workbook, and this resulted in greatly improved relations between them.

Mothers frequently say that the materials in the workbooks help them personally, citing increases in vocabulary, acquisition of new concepts, and exercise in discrimination skills:

> HIPPY has given me a good feeling in body and soul. I sit with my daughter all the time, and I enjoy her learning, and me with her. It also gives me a chance to rest. The program made it possible for me to learn order, education, and patience. I also learned the names of animals, flowers, and all sorts of things.

One teacher reported conversations overheard at a parent-teacher meeting:

> You've got to believe me that from the day my daughter got HIPPY I've learned a lot of sentences that I never in my life knew. I never learned, so I don't have a lot of ideas.

> Well, I'm not ashamed to say in front of all of you that until I received HIPPY for my son I didn't know what a triangle or a square was, or lots of pretty sentences, or about ideas like a straight line and a broken line.

> That's true. Not only do the children progress and learn a lot of new ideas when they are little, but we also get ahead from our children's learning.

Aides as well report changes in the mothers through their involvement with the HIPPY materials. One mother of four, who could neither read nor write, enriched her speaking vocabulary to the point where she was able to take a more active part in helping her son with the workbooks. Another mother told an aide that she had learned how to ask questions. A third illiterate mother, who decided to enter into the learning situation along with her child, helped her son in expression, in working on geometric shapes, and in distinguishing between same-different pictures.

One of the clearest signs of the change that participation in HIPPY produced in the mothers was their increased interest in furthering their own education. While this usually meant learning how to read and write, in some cases it was as basic as learning how to speak the Hebrew language. A mother from Russian Georgia, who never had the opportunity to speak Hebrew with anyone and whose older daughter had been working with the HIPPY child, became convinced that she should learn the language in order to be able to help her child. She was eventually able to take over from the older sibling. A new-immigrant mother from India, who knew so little Hebrew that in her early meetings with the aide she had to rely on her husband to translate for her, enrolled to study Hebrew and succeeded in improving her speaking, reading, and writing dramatically.

A community worker in a town in which HIPPY was active reported that over 50 percent of the students who enrolled in the town's basic education-evening classes were HIPPY mothers. He believed that the unprecedented registration by mothers in new general-enrichment courses suggests that the regular contact between the HIPPY aides and mothers had created a whole new atmosphere—one in which there is "a desire to listen, to progress, to experiment, and to get involved in new programs."

HIPPY aides have been instrumental in involving mothers in community-run literacy programs. One aide, working with a mother aged thirty-five who had four children and who could neither read nor write when she and her child entered HIPPY, "explained to her that there were Hebrew lessons available, and that it would be worth her while to learn and progress so that she would be able to help her son. . . . The mother started the Hebrew lessons, applied herself seriously to them, and began to work with her child on the first workbook, progressed to the second, and so on. Thanks to the Hebrew lessons she can now even write short letters and read things in simple language."

The children, too, generally expressed joy at the novelty of their mother's learning. For some it erased the shame of having an illiterate mother. These children expressed their appreciation in small ways by helping and encouraging the mother whenever possible.

The changes in mothers' attitudes toward education included a heightened interest in the preschool and school activities of their children. Many teachers reported that parents of preschool children were bringing the HIPPY workbooks to class to show what they were doing with their child. The mothers themselves said that they were working more with their children on their lessons and checking with the teachers from time to time to make sure that their children were progressing.

Three of the four mothers on one first-grade parents' committee were found to be HIPPY participants. HIPPY mothers of children in another first-grade class organized a committee to work with the principal and some of the teachers in their school on a program to continue HIPPY when they "graduated" at the end of the year.

All of these changes are not limited to the mothers and their target children. A typical aide's report describes how participation in HIPPY affects all family members: "All the family learn from the workbooks, even the father. Everyone sits together in the evening while the oldest daughter, who is the tutor, questions the child, and they all answer." And, "in the evenings the family turns off the television and sits together while the mother works with the daughter." Still another aide reported that "the children wait for the moment when she [the mother] can sit down with them, and they are angry if she does not." Mothers have commented: "The program has improved general family contact"; "I pay more attention to my children"; "They all like to work together"; "I learned not to belittle small children and what they can do."

There is an interaction effect between participation in HIPPY and relationships within the families. Not only are the family members affected by the program, but their expectations of and behavior toward the participants change as well. The fathers as well as the mothers expect their children to perform better in school. Several mothers reported that they feel more appreciated in their homes. Husbands indicate pride in their wives' new achievements. One husband who said that he was quite happy with the results of the program reported that he has a new appreciation of his wife, and he tries to help out in the home when he can. Another father who does not participate in the activities makes sure that his wife is not disturbed during her work with the HIPPY child. While an observer was there, he took the younger children out, brought in the washing, prepared and offered tea, and got some glue and pencils that his wife and daughter needed for the HIPPY activities. An aide reports of one husband that "he said his wife is making very good progress in language and speech, achievements she would not have made without the program. He very much hopes she will continue for the sake of the daughter now in HIPPY as well as for the other children in the future."

In some cases the change in the mother produces new tensions and problems in the family. Several mothers have reported that their husbands became jealous of them as they learned and advanced. However, the overall impact on the mothers' interactions with their families resulted in new levels of functioning as parents, with the accompanying sense of satisfaction and accomplishment:

> The workbook finally got me to sit *with* my daughter. That's exactly what she said: "Mother you always sit near me but not with me." The program

paved the way for me to work. It's not easy to find the right activities for our young children, and often we even miss the main things.

One of the teachers put it this way:

> HIPPY parents have an important purpose that makes them feel like teachers or instructors who have already acquired experience in dealing with their children's problems; they can help their children and this gives them much satisfaction. For example, when a child answers a question correctly the parents feel that he is bright and clever; when he answers incorrectly, they feel capable of explaining the correct answer to him.

As we gained experience with HIPPY, we became aware of its impact on mothers in a somewhat unexpected area: the reorganization and firming up of household schedules and routines as a result of the new daily activity's being introduced. Aides frequently reported that they had to help the mothers reschedule their household chores and daily activities to allow regular hours for the HIPPY activities. Both mothers and fathers commented on the change that this brought about in their home life, stressing both the increased time spent with the children and the regular participation in an away-from-home group activity.

The significance of this change in home life assumed new proportions as a result of a study by Shamgar-Handelman and Belkin (1979). The researchers, observing and questioning 177 Jerusalem families from a neighborhood in which HIPPY had been functioning for several years, found differences in level of family organization relating to time, space, and the division of labor between the HIPPY and non-HIPPY families and believed that these differences might be related to participation or nonparticipation in HIPPY. Data were gathered on the school achievement of all the children in each family. The combined data on the families and their children were converted to an index of "family scores" (p. 6). Several characteristics of family functioning and organization were then evaluated using the family score as the dependent variable. It was found that "the two main factors in determining the time allocation and organization of a family are the constraints arising from activities of family members outside the home and the patterns of time allocation and organization of the mother" (p. 25). "The more her time is organized according to set routines, the higher the family score" (p. 26).

The overall conclusions of the study indicated that there is "a connection between the family's patterns of organization and functioning and the achievement of its children in school" (p. 44), that the nature of this connection varies from family to family, and that "the more organized and the more efficient the family unit, the higher the children's achievements in school" (p. 45). There was no indication that direct help to children, such as that provided by HIPPY, raises the family score. This may be due to the fact that the family score includes a weighting of grades that increases with advancement in school years; since the HIPPY children are all young, their scores have a minimal effect on the overall findings. In addition, the HIPPY children comprised only a small part of the total population studied.

Information on whether some of the changes that occur in HIPPY children can be traced to a change in overall family organization will be available when the Shamgar-Handelman and Belkin data are reanalyzed to examine the differences between HIPPY and non-HIPPY families.

The changes in the self-perception of HIPPY mothers were not limited to their views of themselves in relation to their families. As a result of the group meetings and activities, there was also a change in how they saw themselves vis-à-vis the community. In discussing this change, they tended to emphasize the number of new friends they made at group meetings. They also stressed that the sharing of ideas, the enrichment programs, the projects, and the special activities provided a pleasant atmosphere in which to make discoveries about themselves and their children. One aide, in her report on a particular mother, said, "She loves to come to the group meetings at the club, she is present on all excursions, and she takes part in the handicrafts programs. She is always organized and jokes and is happy to get out of the house—something she never did before."

A coordinator reported on a young immigrant mother who had not made any friends and was having so much trouble in adjusting to Israel that she spoke of returning to her country of origin. The links created with other mothers at the HIPPY group meetings gave her the impetus to join other groups as well. The coordinator felt that HIPPY had helped her to take the first step in trying to improve her condition.

The data collected on various aspects of HIPPY's impact on mothers led us to believe that mothers who work with the program may very likely undergo a general change in self-concept. From a small study in one city where HIPPY operated (Alon 1980), we found that this does indeed appear to be true. Alon administered an Israeli adaptation of the Tennessee Self-Concept Scale (Fitts 1965; Frankel 1976) to all the mothers who joined HIPPY in a particular year (N = 50). They were tested upon entry and were reexamined at the end of the first and second years of participation. Alon's analysis was structured to measure the change in self-concept effected by participation in HIPPY. Three groups were identified for this purpose—mothers who dropped out before the end of the first year, mothers who dropped out during the second year, and those who remained in the program for the full two years—with length of participation considered the independent variable. Differences among the three groups were found to be significant ($p < 0.01$) for all eight subscales of the test, suggesting, according to Alon, that participation in HIPPY appears to improve the self-concept of the adult participants as measured by this test and, further, that the predominant change appears to take place during the first year.

Examination of the two groups of mothers who did not complete the program indicates that the early dropouts differ from those who left during the second year. The latter exhibited changes in self-concept similar to those exhibited by mothers who completed the full two years.

Alon suggests that changes in the mother's self-concept will effect her family in general, as well as the HIPPY child in particular. When viewed in combination with HIPPY's impact on the mothers' views of education, on their sense of success in the program, and on their increased competence as parents and community members, it appears that HIPPY has a broad and effective impact on those who elect to join the program.

Impact on Aides

While not discounting its effect on the target children, on their mothers, and on other family members, there is still no doubt that HIPPY's greatest impact is on the aides who work with HIPPY families. From their own reports on themselves, as well as from the coordinators' evaluations and reports from all others who have observed the aides over time, it appears that the aides benefit most from involvement in HIPPY. Although this was not one of the effects predicted for HIPPY, it might have been expected. The aides, who are members of the community in which they work, partake of everything given to the program mothers. In addition, they benefit from being taught by a professional, are required to repeat that which they have been taught many times each week, and in their work with mothers find themselves in situations where they must clearly articulate what they have learned. This experience of highly motivated learning combined with frequent review and clarification of newly learned materials produces highly visible changes in the aides' level of understanding and performance.

There are now about 650 aides working in various locations throughout Israel. Their recruitment is sometimes difficult in the first year of HIPPY's introduction into a community, whose residents know nothing about the program or the role of the aide. Once the program is underway, however, there is no problem in recruiting the growing number of aides needed to work with the increasing number of families, since the HIPPY mothers themselves provide a ready source of new aides, considering it an honor to be chosen for the position.

There appear to be good reasons for the aides' success in and enjoyment of their new roles. They earn a small but respectable salary during hours that enable them to continue their functions as mothers and homemakers.

Their new job brings them new relationships, new skills, and a new sense of competence.

In speaking of their early problems with mothers, they indicate how they learned to cope. One aide who had to overcome a tremendous amount of hostility from a particular mother succeeded in working with her by bringing her a new workbook each week in spite of her apparent disinterest in the program. "Today," she said, "after a long time and many struggles, this mother is one of the best. She is very diligent, and I very much enjoy coming to her house, seeing her interest in the workbook, and the pleasure with which she goes through the materials with her children."

Another aide was faced with a mother who expressed resentment over the fact that the aide, with no more education or experience than she, should presume to try to teach her how to work with her child. By admitting her inexperience and explaining that she was only trying to teach a system that she herself had learned from the coordinator, the aide won the mother's trust. She said, "Today, after two years, when I review those years, I can't believe that Mrs. D. is the same woman. She's now one of the best mothers in the program. More than that, I have become one of her closest friends. . . . She's one of those to whom I can turn and tell anything, good or bad."

The aides also exhibit a sensitivity to the differences in the mothers with whom they work. For example, they differentiate between mothers by age: "In general, it's easier, and more pleasant to work with the older mothers. They have a more serious attitude, and they are ready to give their full cooperation. Young mothers sometimes stop the aide and say they understand everything."

Speaking of the differences between working with mothers in groups and at home, they say: "The talks with the coordinators and at group meetings release a mother from worry, since the problems she has are shared by other mothers and she sees that she is not alone in her anxieties"; "At home the mother concentrates better."

The aides often find themselves offering information to mothers, encouraging them to join new activities, and providing them with help outside the area of HIPPY activities through the coordinator. As one aide said, "At work the aide is a listener for the mothers. She hears family problems and refers them to the coordinator, who gets them to the right address." An observer, reporting on the aide's interactions with mothers, had the following to say:

> The aide asked the mother if she were taking her child to the theater with the other mothers and their children, stressing the importance of such an outing for all involved.
>
> The aide asked the mother why the child's eyes were red and swollen. When the mother explained that the child went to bed late, got up early, and

went to his parents' bed, the aide tried to help convince the child of the advantages of going to bed early. . . . When this mother complained about the weaknesses of her eldest son as a pupil, the aide used this as the basis to encourage her in her work with the target child.

The aides speak of their new sense of social competence and ability to deal with unusual situations. One aide arrived at one of the homes at the appointed hour and knocked at the door. Although she could hear noise and activity inside, the door was not opened. When she called out to ask why they were not opening the door, they answered, "We haven't finished the workbook yet." The aide laughed and, after convincing them to open after all, reassured them that aides are not policemen for the program. Such things happen because, "after all, we are all human." Another aide, responsible for a twenty-three-year-old Indian mother of four who could neither read nor write, developed a system whereby she explained and read out the story for the week, moving about and dramatizing all the actions in the story in order to clarify the words and thereby making it possible for the mother to tell the story to her children.

A major source of the aides' satisfaction in their work comes from their sense of fulfillment in providing mothers and children with a service:

Sometimes a mother comes to my house and says: "Listen, I didn't understand something," and I sit and explain it to her. Then I feel that I gave that mother something so that she will be able to give something to her child to help him progress.

I enjoy hearing the mother tell of her son's improvement since joining HIPPY. He talks to her about all kinds of things, and she feels that he loves her more. She feels closer to him as well. I was very excited when she told me of these changes in her child.

One aide told of a shy, introverted four-year-old boy, the son of illiterate parents, who seemed to have severe difficulties in communication. The aide, through the coordinator, arranged for the child to work with a speech therapist. She also arranged for the boy's older sister to work with him on the HIPPY materials. As he made slow but real progress in his work and his speech, his self-confidence increased. The aide concluded, "I, who followed his progress over such a long period of time, find his development wonderful. I love hearing him speak, answering my questions, and revealing curiosity and interest in many things."

Aides' satisfaction in making a contribution is generally combined with their satisfaction in the changes in themselves:

I have a feeling of making a contribution to the group, my self-confidence has grown, and I have learned patience and understanding.

The fact that I get out of the daily routine of the kitchen and housework, and get to know nice mothers and talk to them . . . the fact that I contribute a little knowledge to them, gives me much satisfaction.

The program has made me more independent, more sure of myself, more aware of exactly what I can contribute to someone else.

I've learned to take advantage of my free time and to get organized both inside and outside the house.

This program developed my general education. I learned to express myself better, both in speaking and in writing. This work is with people. During my work I've learned to treat each person differently.

Before I went to work I was nervous and tense. Today I'm relaxed. All my tension is in my work, and I return home relaxed.

An aide who is mother of six children herself reported that whereas before the program she did not leave the house, she has now made friends and met other people. Her husband, who used to prefer that she stay home with the children, reacted to her progress by beginning to help out in the house.

Aides feel that the changes in themselves relate to their roles as wives and mothers as well:

The program changed my relationship with my husband. Now I sit with him and we talk about the improvement in the mothers and how each one receives me. He, too, values HIPPY.

Evening work is a problem for my family, but the big plus is that my husband now assumes more of his share of family obligations. He feeds the children and puts them to bed. For me that's the greatest thing. And I know that, although they keep it a secret, he and the children are proud of me.

The program has given me knowledge and skills for sitting with my children in our free time.

My daughter is proud of me, and the program helped me to know my children better.

Approval for their new status came not only from the family. After interviewing the HIPPY aides in one program, a university student reported that they felt they were contributing to the community and that their role in the program was important. It gave them status, which is important to them. One aide cited with pride the fact that now her neighbors view her as a source of information and a figure of authority. One aide stated it succinctly:

Today, when a child meets me in the street and calls out after me, "Teacher, I have finished learning in the workbook; could you bring me another?'' I am very pleased to hear him call to me this way. I am a simple housewife who began to work and to go out of the house because of HIPPY. I feel wonderful. Until yesterday I was this boy's neighbor; today I am his teacher.

The aide's role is relatively easy to learn, and it provides a good deal of reinforcement and opportunity for personal and occupational growth. In the first three years she learns new materials, meets new people, and, as the program expands, learns to assume new roles within the team of aides. At the end of the third year, upon entering a new round of instruction, many aides express the desire to further their own education. This has been encouraged by individual counseling and guidance on study programs that will advance them toward high school certification and open channels for advanced or specialized studies, as well as by offering them special enrichment courses, in cooperation with such services as the Department of Adult Education or local psychological services, which deal with children's literature, child development, human behavior, and play. The aides are enthusiastic about these programs organized especially for them. Attendance is high even when it involves extra time or their having to pay for transportation to and from the course.

Not all aides complete the full three years. About one in five serves one year or less. The reasons for leaving are pregnancy (the prime cause), illness, family pressure, more lucrative job opportunities, and leaving the neighborhood. The fact that they no longer work as aides, however, does not mean that these women withdraw from HIPPY. Most of those who stop working as aides remain in the program as mothers of HIPPY children. And they are taught by their former colleagues or even by their own replacement. Interestingly enough, the shift in roles has caused very few problems.

We have recently begun to cope with the problem of aides who we feel have served long enough and should be phased out of the program of service. These women generally no longer have HIPPY-aged children and therefore may not have the same freshness of approach needed to interact with client-mothers. This is not easy because few other jobs open to them provide the kind of involvement and flexibility of hours offered by working with HIPPY. We are therefore beginning to explore new employment possibilities for aides. Several school principals have employed former aides to work in new paraprofessional positions in their schools. Social work departments in some communities have taken on former aides as community aides to work alongside professional social workers. Because the use of paraprofessionals in these fields is new in Israel, the success of the aides in these initial ventures will be closely monitored, and implications for the wider use of aides will be drawn over the next few years.

Impact on the Community

Community expectations for HIPPY primarily are based on improving the
school achievement of its children. Since this is a somewhat long-term
objective, the allocation of a relatively large percentage of its budget to
HIPPY is based on the expectation that it will work better than other programs. According to one head of a local department of education:

> HIPPY provides organized written materials, which eases our task of
> administering the program, as well as the mother's task in working with her
> child. It engages about 180 families in many varied activities, something we
> do not often see in programs which cost a lot more money.

As HIPPY takes hold, local community administrators find that it brings
additional benefits in terms of its use of local personnel and its activation of
mothers in the education of their children:

> We have succeeded in something that we have wanted to do for many
> years. No outside teachers, volunteers, or tutors come to teach in the
> homes. . . . Today mothers are taking back for themselves the honored
> position of educators for their children. We have succeeded in having the
> mothers guided by women from our own community.

Although kindergarten and first-grade teachers are not actively involved
in HIPPY, we frequently receive spontaneous reports from them on what
they view as the impact of the program. They see HIPPY as reinforcing
kindergarten learning and broadening children's knowledge in a variety of
important areas. They are particularly impressed by the way in which the
HIPPY mothers work with their children:

> The children, full of impressions of new experiences and of excitement,
> come and tell about how they have learned from their mothers, that their
> mothers taught them, that this is the day on which they are to receive new
> workbooks. The special attention they receive from their parents brings
> great joy to their hearts.

> The program teaches parents to be involved in their child's progress.

A first-grade teacher says that HIPPY prepares the children for school:

> The program provides new concepts and strengthens those which the child
> already knows. Vocabularies grow and oral expression improves; the
> child's horizons are widened, and he learns skills in cutting, pasting, color-
> ing, and drawing lines. In short, it prepares him for school.

The children's own excitement about the program is cited by many.
Mothers speak of their child's enthusiasm for the workbook. Aides tell

stories of children who sit on the stairs outside their apartments waiting for them to arrive with a new workbook. Teachers have recorded observations of the children discussing their aides, their workbook, how much they have done, and who is doing best. The teachers welcome this kind of competitive arousal to new learning tasks.

An ever-increasing number of communities in Israel are requesting that HIPPY be implemented in some of their neighborhoods. While its average growth of over 75 percent annually over the past five years has been, to a large extent, due to government financing, the fact that it is a program selected from among several possibilities and that it is among the more expensive of these programs indicates some sort of match between the communities' needs and the program in operation.

6

Assessment of the Implementation of HIPPY

Purpose

The implementation of a research program frequently involves the kinds of adaptive changes that bring about substantive changes in the original program. When this happens, the field operation, although it may bear the name of the original project, no longer resembles the original model in terms of the nature of the work actually being carried out. The possibility existed that changes of this sort had been occurring in HIPPY during its four years of rapid expansion. The changes may have been so subtle that they eluded our system of information feedback. If such changes had taken place, it would be important to note this, both in terms of evaluating HIPPY's impact and in any consideration of the factors that had been suggested in the original model as being promotive of program success.

In the winter of 1978 Chava Cohen of the Research Institute undertook a field of study of how HIPPY was actually being implemented at that time. Cohen, who observed and interviewed HIPPY participants throughout Israel, arrived at the general conclusion that HIPPY today closely resembles the model projected and, further, that there is reason to believe that the model will continue to resist changes.

Design

The design for Cohen's study involved observation and talking with all levels of participants drawn from a sample of HIPPY locations that were representative of the country-wide program. The six locations chosen included one large urban, one small urban, three development towns (one in each geographic region of the country), and one regional cluster of villages.

Two local coordinators were selected for the study in each of the two cities; one coordinator was studied in each of the other locations. The two aides selected from each coordinator's team were chosen so that the number of aides studied would be representative of the number of aides teaching each of the three HIPPY ages.

The aides were representative of aides in the general HIPPY population. They ranged in age from thirty to thirty-five, were all of Afro-Asian background, had completed eight to ten years of schooling, and any pre-

97

vious salaried work had been in industry, sales, child care, and housework. Twelve of the aides had three children each; the other four had five to seven children each.

Three of the families in each aide's care were visited. Individual meetings were then held with the aides and the local coordinators and later with the regional coordinators and the national coordinator. A summary of the overall design is presented in table 6-1.

Procedure

Fifty mothers were interviewed initially, although only forty-eight of these were observed for the study. All but one was of Afro-Asian origin, and of these six were born in Israel. Thirty-four (68 percent) of the mothers were between twenty-four and thirty years old; sixteen (32 percent) were thirty to forty years old; and one (2 percent) was over forty. Ten of the mothers (20 percent) had no education at all; thirty-two (64 percent) had six to eight years of school; six (12 percent) had up to ten years; and two (4 percent) were high-school graduates. Half of the mothers were full-time housewives; the other half worked in local industry, as saleswomen in shops, in housework, or on their own farms.

The fathers were generally employed in industry near the home or as craftsmen. A few were members of the police or the armed forces. Family size ranged from two to three children (thirty families, 60 percent); four to seven children (sixteen families, 32 percent); and eight to eleven children (four families, 8 percent). Half of the mothers had been raised in families of seven to nine children.

The fact that all the data in this study were collected by the researcher may render the findings somewhat subjective, however, questionnaires and observation guide sheets were used wherever possible in order to ensure a degree of standardization in the collection of the data.

Table 6-1
Design for Evaluation of Field Implementation

Location	Number of Local Coordinators	Number of Aides	Number of Mothers
Large city	2	4	12
Small city	2	4	12
Northern town	1	2	6
Central town	1	2	6
Southern town	1	2	6
Village region	1	2	6
Total	8	16	48

In each location the researcher first met the coordinators and aides during their regular weekly training session. She described the study, explaining that her primary interest was in seeing how all the contacts are made and how the program works at each level. She also assured them that her study did not include evaluation at any level. After a brief discussion, the researcher remained at the training session as an observer. At the end of the session she made appointments to accompany the two aides selected for the study on their visits to families.

Visits were made to the first three families on each aide's schedule for the day in question. The mothers received no prior notice of the researcher's visit. Upon arrival in the home, the researcher explained her presence, indicating that her purpose was general observation, not assessment. She then observed the aide and the mother working together on the weekly workbook. At the end of this visit, she arranged to return at a time when the mother would be working on the HIPPY materials with her child. After mother and child were observed working together for from fifteen to twenty minutes, the mother was interviewed for one to two hours using a semistructured questionnaire.

After the researcher had observed and interviewed all of one aide's mothers, she met with the aide in her home for a long (one to two hours) talk, probing for information concerning the aide's views of herself, her role, and the program. When this procedure had been repeated with the second aide and her families, a meeting was arranged with the local coordinator. This was a fully open-ended discussion (lasting two to four hours) in which all possible aspects of the coordinator's work were explored. Similar discussions took place with the regional and national coordinators toward the end of the study.

Findings

Cohen's primary finding is that HIPPY's current operation closely resembles that of the original model. Children are doing the workbook activities regularly. They are instructed by their mothers who are taught what to do in weekly sessions with a community aide. The aides meet in weekly training and guidance sessions with the professional coordinator, and the coordinator assumes full responsibility for the total operation of the local program.

Whereas the mode of operation of HIPPY in the communities studied was strikingly similar, there were strong indications of differences in the quality of operation. Evidence of these differences came from interviews with the participants rather than observation of their activity in the program, which led Cohen to examine the possibility of the existence of two different dimensions to the program: the operational and the interactive. Examination of the interactive dimension yielded information on differences among the local programs.

In her introduction to the examination of the differences among the HIPPY programs studied, Cohen discusses the contextual framework within which the whole program exists, suggesting that every set of experiences occurs with a given context and the context of a program has direct bearing on its importance to the participants. The three contextual dimensions suggested to be of importance in analyzing HIPPY are the national, the sociocultural, and the institutional contexts.

As a nonpolitical educational program that incorporates self-help both in its structure and in its content, HIPPY meets a national as well as a community need. Its stated objective—that of enabling the weaker elements in society to gain strength and join the mainstream—invests it with high value. Reports from the field indicating its success increase its value for the community and for the educational establishment in general. This, in turn, has produced increased readiness to invest budget and personnel in the program.

In its sociocultural context, HIPPY offers hope for change in an area of prime concern: the social gap in Israel. This is a reality that the society is trying to cope with, and HIPPY addresses itself to this problem. In terms of the participants, however, HIPPY meets more than a social need. One of the characteristics of the educationally disadvantaged is the gap between level of achievement and level of expectation for both themselves and their children. Their somewhat optimistic though often unrealistic view of their future provides them with a strong impetus to participate in any program that they believe will help them achieve these goals. HIPPY's clientele are thus preprimed to be willing participants.

Cohen terms the institutional settings in which HIPPY functions the parent-institution and the adult-education contexts. She suggests that the Hebrew University represents a status framework for adult-education institutions. It is held in high esteem by both parents and communities, and its involvement with the parent institution increases the value of this institution in the eyes of all participants. The high status ascribed to HIPPY pulls together the many potential services and subsidiary institutions in the community at large, all of which view themselves as gaining by their association with the program. This, in turn, contributes to its further success.

The high value placed on participation in HIPPY lends strength to the program but does not preclude differences in the quality of involvement of the participants. In the retroactive analysis involved in examining this aspect, Cohen found that any weakness in the chain affects all of the subsequent links. Conversely one could locate the source of weakenss in the functioning of one link by examining the previous links. The most persistent area of weakness in the chain effect was in communication between one operative level and another. The highest level in which weaknesses of this kind were found was that of the local coordinator.

Cohen found the relationship between the local coordinator and the aides to be crucial to the operation of HIPPY. She suggests that the successful carrying out of the coordinator's role requires that person to possess communication skills and a deep understanding of the dynamics of interpersonal relations. Although in the case of the aides the presence of these attributes acts to increase the potential for success, in the case of the coordinator they are essential, for she cannot function in her work without them.

Two of the local coordinators studied, who were new to their jobs, were having trouble taking over from the well-functioning coordinators they replaced. In both cases, the aides complained as well, and there appeared to be a general drop in morale. In one of these cases examination of data collected revealed that the coordinator had serious doubts about the efficacy of the program. She found it hard to relax with it an let the process prove itself, trying instead to create a tight supervisory structure over the aides. She demanded loyalty to the program and adherence to a set standard of rules that reflected her own interpretation of what should be happening. This coordinator might have been successful in her approach had she also been able to transmit the sense of mission that should have gone with it. In its absence, however, the aides merely felt put upon, and they expressed their hostility in disillusionment with the work.

The case of the second problematic coordinator was somewhat different. Although she fully believed that the program works and was well worth her time, she lacked basic skills in interpersonal relationships, especially with aides. Her lack of confidence in her own role as leader confused the aides, especially when her attempts at democratic interaction dropped to the level of competition with them. The aides' reaction was one of discomfort and withdrawal, making her acceptance as their leader even more difficult.

Cohen strongly suggests that the level on which the coordinator functions accounts for most of HIPPY's success or lack of it. Although they are all professionals who have been successfully involved in some form of work in the community, the local coordinators enter HIPPY with high anxiety and little knowledge of the realities facing them along with their high hopes. They quickly find themselves at the center of an actively functioning program for which they must provide support and guidance while receiving relatively little of either from the community. (This is due to the self-contained nature of HIPPY, which, although it has been chosen by the community, is largely independent of it in the early stages of implementation.)

The coordinators reported that their first year was far harder than they had expected. The factors that sustained them during this period seem to be their belief in the program, their sense of mission, and the positive feedback from the field indicating increasing success and enthusiasm on the part of both mothers and aides. Cohen made a strong recommendation that some of the coordinator's sense of isolation be alleviated through ongoing, regular enrichment sessions that would provide them with new ideas and help them to build new skills in coping with the less-structured—and more frequently taxing—aspects of the program.

With regard to the aides, Cohen found that they are extremely proud of themselves, their work, and the changes that their work has brought into their lives. Their horizons are widened, and their new sense of accomplishment produces a drive for further personal advancement through education.

The minor changes that Cohen found occasionally in the program were not of the dimension likely to produce substantive changes in the model. She suggests that key factors determine the stability and replicability of HIPPY and, further, that the presence of these factors accounts for the similarity and success of the program in the various communities around the country.

The factors may be broken down into the known elements in the program such as the materials, the organizational structure, and the lines of communication; and the basic factors beyond these that contribute to the stability of the program: belief in the efficacy of the materials, the sense of mission vis-à-vis the community, success in administration, comments by participants indicating their gratitude and a sense of cohesiveness that stimulates loyalty.

Cohen suggests that certain other elements of HIPPY in the area of interpersonal dynamics also have a strong bearing on its stability: the provision of a forum (intimate or group) for the expression of feelings and the exchange of ideas, the inclusion of the participants in some of the decision-making processes, and the recognition of and affirmation that changes occur in the self-concept and performance of all participants.

Cohen suggests that the structure of the HIPPY model minimized substantive changes. Although it provides for the rigid adherence to a basic core of activities that makes it convenient and easy for the participants, it also encompasses the flexibility and adaptability necessary for it to be adapted to the needs of local groups. For example, although the activities in HIPPY groups are scheduled as part of the overall program, they acquire their specific content and form only as a result of the interaction among coordinator, aides, and mothers in the different settings of interview, tutorials, small groups, and larger groups. Each contact between participants has the potential of creating new factors, which will affect future interactions between all participants. This process, Cohen suggests, is the primary reason why HIPPY has been able to root itself in a variety of settings.

HIPPY has been growing over the years, and growth means change. New community and staff needs have been met as they arose at every step of the growth process. This process of adaptation has produced new dimensions for the program, which in turn have provided new inputs for the participants and the community. Without this interaction and reciprocal change, which occurred without affecting the basic core of this program, HIPPY would have come into conflict with community needs and demands and would not have continued to operate. Cohen concludes that the flexible aspect of HIPPY provides protection for its basic structure and allows for a balance between the demands of the model and those of the absorbing community.

7

Current Status and Implication for the Future of HIPPY

The periodic evaluation of an ongoing program enables its designers to take stock of the current situation, as well as to anticipate new developments and plan for changes. In the case of HIPPY, extensive testing in the field plus evaluative studies over the years not only have provided justification for its continuation and growth but have contributed to our understanding of the feasibility of the program. We know more about the practicality of the program, and we have new bases for discussing its desirability or suitability. In our examination of the feasibility of HIPPY, we will summarize the main features of the program and then discuss them in terms of recently published findings related to the implementation of innovative educational programs.

Practicality

Although the basic HIPPY package is highly structured, quite rigid, and easily applied, the group program allows for a good deal of flexibility and adaptation to local situations. The dual nature of the program contributes to the success of implementation.

Early studies of the effects that structure has on the success of a program indicate that the more structured a program, the more effective it is (Van De Riet et al. 1968-1969). This conclusion was borne out later when evaluation of the implementation of federally funded innovative educational programs in the United States yielded firm evidence that structure in programs increases the success of implementation (Berman and McLaughlin 1978). In their analysis of the factors affecting the implementation of these programs, Berman and McLaughlin concluded that "what a project *was* mattered less than how it was done" (p. vii). They found that effective implementation strategies included concrete and extended training, regular meetings focusing on practical problems, teacher participation in project decisions, teacher observation of similar projects, and local development of materials.

Although Berman and McLaughlin arrived at their criteria on the basis of innovative programs in the classroom and HIPPY is a home-based program, the strategies used in HIPPY meet their criteria for effectiveness. The training program is concrete, specific, and runs the length of the program.

The regular group meetings built into the program for all levels of participants allow for discussion of practical problems, decision making concerning ongoing group program, and, when necessary, development of new group program ideas. The regional meetings, at which the functioning of HIPPY in a particular location may be the subject of repeated discussion, provide for an exchange of information and ideas in a manner that approximates the observation of different programs.

Examination of the variety of settings into which HIPPY has been introduced indicates that the process of mutual adaptation, which Berman and McLaughlin suggest occurs in the successful implementation of innovative programs, has been at work. The standard model was created in a large urban neighborhood where the target families were densely concentrated. Subsequent implementations of HIPPY, however, have been carried out in settings as varied as agricultural villages, small towns, and even Arab refugee camps. (HIPPY has been operating in these camps since 1975. The material has been translated and the program adapted to local conditions. The aides in the camps are young unmarried teachers who volunteer their time to work within their family clans.)

HIPPY is most difficult to implement in agricultural villages. Although there are no more than six hundred HIPPY families in such villages, our experience with them to date has helped us to define the limits of the program's adaptability. There are generally only eight to twelve four year olds in any one village, which means that four or more villages must be combined to make up one local program, with the office of the local coordinator generally situated some distance from them all. Thus the cost of HIPPY rises considerably for these villages when the burden of transportation is added. A no-less-important obstacle stems from the fact that the selection of aides is made difficult by the limited number of candidates in each village. Also the intensity of relations among neighbors in these small communities often results in the best-suited candidate from our point of view not being chosen because she will not be accepted by the target mothers. In addition, communication between coordinators and aides is much more difficult here than in other settings since most of the aides have no telephones. And from our own experience as well as from Cohen's (1980) observations, it is apparent that this communication factor has been central to HIPPY's adaptability in its various settings.

The group aspect of HIPPY and the flexibility it provides has activated the community involvement with the program, producing the kind of mutual adaptation and adjustment conducive to healthy program implementation. There is often a tendency, however, for a successful program to be so well adopted by the community that the original structure is lost in the process. The HIPPY local coordinators have been instrumental in maintaining the fine line between community participation and community takeover.

Another source of HIPPY's effectiveness is the length of the program. The three-year duration provides enough time for change to take place. It is only in the second year of participation that mothers begin to show signs of full involvement in the program, that their self-concept improves, and that they develop increased sensitivity to their children and their children's needs. This corresponds to findings reported by Barletta et al. (1978), who say that "it takes about two years of parent participation before an impact occurs" (p. 75). Children also need at least two years in the program for it to affect their level of school achievement. Gordon et al. (1977), who found that "the longer the participation the greater the gains" (p. 117), also suggest that the age of intervention is less important than the length of program participation. Although she agrees with this basic premise, Clarke-Stewart (1979) finds no evidence to justify continuing such programs for more than three years.

The third factor in the successful implementation of HIPPY is its appeal to all those involved. The Ministry of Education feels secure in expending a relatively large portion of its welfare program budget and a good deal of effort on the expansion of the program because of its ongoing relationship with the Hebrew University.

From the community point of view, HIPPY promises and produces four positive results: well-organized and responsive groups of mothers with whom it is possible to conduct a variety of community education and action programs; aides who are candidates for future community leadership roles; children who start school with a clear head start; and the sense of satisfaction in accomplishing these objectives with local rather than outside experts. The enthusiastic response of mothers, aides, and coordinators clearly indicates that their expectations have been met. No doubt there are areas in which the program has little if any effect, but there appears to be a match between current needs and expectations of all levels of participants and what HIPPY accomplishes in the field.

The national funding of HIPPY spurred its implementation and growth. The escalation of a substantial budget very soon after the original research study was completed and as information was still being gathered on the implementation in communities scattered around the country meant that we could concentrate on issues of substance, structure, and administration rather than funding.

The expansion of HIPPY was designed to allow for gradual growth, with close monitoring of changes and problems as they occurred, thereby making it possible to provide the adaptive changes necessary in the program's administration. The monitored growth program also allows local authorities to evaluate their allocation of funds to the program. Since the operation of HIPPY was discontinued in only two of the eighty sites in which it has been set up, it became known that money invested in this program was money well spent. With this kind of recommendation, plus national funding, the program could have expanded more rapidly if we had not made a concerted effort to keep to our schedule of monitored growth.

Program Desirability and Suitability

The desirability of a program such as HIPPY must be assessed on the basis of the kinds of changes it produces in the child, the mother, the family, and the community. When reviewing the desirability of HIPPY for children, it is helpful to look at the program in the context of data pertaining to other recent enrichment programs for preschool children. Most of these data have come from the United States.

The American experience has focused on providing disadvantaged children with a one-year early group experience, with or without home-based activities. The first findings in the evaluation of preschool programs indicated that children did indeed learn in this preschool year. These reports were soon overshadowed by follow-up studies, however, indicating that the gains made seem to vanish within a few years of school entry. In the decade between the publication of these studies and the Lazar report in 1977, the efficacy of the Head Start programs was seriously questioned. But with the publication of the Lazar report, the Head Start preschool year for disadvantaged children was shown to have a beneficial effect on the children's feelings about themselves as students as well as on their school performance and to be cost-effective to the community over time.

In Israel there has been no question as to the value of preschool: 97 percent of all four year olds and 89 percent of all three year olds attended government-supported preschools in 1978 (Bielecky and Egozi 1978). Yet the preschool experience alone is not enough to keep the disadvantaged children moving successfully through the school years.

The school performance of the children in the original HIPPY study, measured into the ninth grade, indicates that these children have been helped by their HIPPY experience. Since the children in the replication and implementation studies are still quite young, the findings on them are less conclusive to date. Nevertheless, the data on school achievement to date indicate that participation in HIPPY has been of help in the early school years. The long-term data now being gathered will indicate the strength of HIPPY's impact on these children.

Children like participating in HIPPY. Evidence from the field repeatedly indicates that they enjoy the program itself and bask in the attention that participation affords them. HIPPY can therefore be said to provide early home-based enrichment experiences that enable children in preschools to have an increased chance of school success and an increased sense of involvement in educational activity.

The decision to involve mothers actively in the educational enrichment of their children was made on the basis of two major objectives: to capitalize on the mother's role as the natural tutor of her child and to activate change in the mother in order to expand her potential as an educator. The efficacy of this approach has been borne out by findings on home-based enrichment programs in the United States.

Vopava and Royce (1978) state that programs in which parents were actively involved produced better results for the participating children. In her review of the effects of parent-training programs on children, Clarke-Stewart (1979) points to the consistency of such results: "It is clear that parent-training programs can have immediate effects on children's intellectual performance and development" (p. 85). It is less clear whether they have any effect on the participating mothers.

The fact that parent enthusiasm for home-based programs has been widely documented (Zigler 1978) has been used to justify their continuation. Certainly popularity is one measure of suitability, but the continuation of any program should be based on additional criteria. The Home Start programs, which followed Head Start by several years, worked from the premise that change in mothers would bring about changes in their children. Although documentation is sparse in this area, O'Keefe (1979) cites increases in the teaching of reading and writing skills, in providing books and playthings, and in reading to their children as indicative that Home Start effects change in mothers. Goldberg (1978) found that although mothers who learn effective approaches to teaching their children do have a positive effect, the results are more productive when mothers focus on general learning rather than on the academic preparation of their children for school. General knowledge and level of interest appear to be of greater importance than the acquisition of specific skills.

There is increasing evidence that the change that occurs in parents results from the program itself, as well as from change in their child's behavior. Emphasizing this point, Clarke-Stewart (1979) points out that "gains are greatest when *both* parent and child are active in the program . . . since changes in the child's behavior can lead to changes in the parents" (p. 96). In this interrelationship both mother and child are reinforced for the changes that occur as a result of their participation in a program.

One of our underlying assumptions in structuring HIPPY activities for mothers to use with their children was that the child's chances of succeeding with the activities would be increased by good programming and that children would learn and change as they progressed through the program. Because the mothers are active participants in this process, the way in which they interact with their children could be expected to change accordingly, and this would also bring about change in themselves.

From reports by HIPPY mothers and aides, as well as from coordinators and other community representatives, it appears that mothers who participate for two or more years do undergo changes in behavior and attitudes. The most evident are:

1. They view their children differently in that they perceive them more as individuals, express more warmth to the target child, and evince more interest in their children's education.
2. The regularity and intensity of their participation increases over time. They are more likely to complete the weekly assignment with their children, to attend the group meetings more regularly, and, once there, to participate more actively.
3. Their view of themselves changes, and this change is accompanied by a change in how they are viewed by their families.
4. There is an increased participation in away-from-home activities. More mothers seek and participate in educational programs for their own advancement. They are more active in community activities.

The desirability of HIPPY for communities is based on three factors: the effect on children, the response of participants, and the ease of administration.

Research findings on children's educational achievement, together with the positive reactions and comments by teachers and other local personnel, provide educational decision makers with the justification for funding HIPPY in their communities. The apparent match between community expectations and needs and HIPPY's impact on children, mothers, and aides provides a strong rationale for community implementation. The positive response of the participants in the program substantiates the local committee's decision to select HIPPY for implementation.

However innovative a program may be, its ultimate value is reduced if it is difficult to implement or requires the creation of extensive new staffing, administrative, or supervisory structures. HIPPY is convenient in this respect: it provides clear guidelines for implementation by local authorities, its staff is drawn from a local population of otherwise unemployed women, and all ongoing guidance and supervision is provided by the Research Institute.

Future of HIPPY

HIPPY's success over the years and the promise for its future expansion calls for serious review of the program within the general educational framework. There are some basic ethical questions relating to the use of the home in educational intervention, and the educational establishment must review them regularly in the process of decision making.

In their hopes for parent-education programs, educators assume that children's performance and behavior in large part is due to some aspect of their parents' interactions with them and that middle-class parents do activities with their children that are conducive to school success. Therefore if the parents of disadvantaged children were taught these activities, their interactions with their children would become more conducive to school success. This is, itself, based on the assumptions that we can pinpoint what it is that middle-class parents do with their children and that we can teach the parents of disadvantaged children to do these activities. Neither of these secondary assumptions is wholly realistic.

Although a growing body of knowledge concerns the factors involved in children's success in school, few definitive studies have examined these critical factors. Further any program that seriously considers teaching parents new behaviors would have to meet basic requirements of learning psychology: it would have to state its objectives clearly for the learner; to secure the learner's active participation in the process; to provide a variety of experiences concerning, and repeated practice of, the behaviors it wishes him or her to learn; and to include ongoing feedback on the learner's performance. If these assumptions were to be found valid—that is, if we knew what it is that we want to teach parents if we could indeed change their behavior in these areas—then two further questions arise: do current parent-education programs have a potential for effecting these changes, and having effected the changes, is there reason to expect that they will produce the desired changes in the children?

In her review of parental effects on child development, Clarke-Stewart (1979) says that parent-education programs have presumed an unfounded chain of influence whereby program curriculum brings about changes in parental behavior that result in gains in child development. She does not believe that the existence of support for the relationship between parent behavior and child development proves that "changes in parent or child development can be induced simply through programs that increase parents' knowledge about child rearing or child development or that modify only a minimum number of behaviors" (p. 96). The critical factor in producing such change appears to be the participation of both parent and child. It is this situation that creates a positive interactive effect and is the most effective one for bringing about desired changes. Programs that do not incorporate the child have little reason to expect that they will have any impact on her or him.

Another potentially dangerous aspect of the promise offered by parent-education programs in general is that they are built on the premise that the child's success (or failure) in school is determined as much by the parents as by the school. If parents of disadvantaged children participate in parent-education programs under the assumption that they are contributing to their child's future success in so doing and their participation does not bring about changes in the child's school performance, their increased feelings of inadequacy and failure will result in a pulling back from further contact with the educational establishment. To the extent that parent-school communication is important for stability and continuity in the child's school career, the parent-education program thereby will have proven to be countereffective for the child.

In HIPPY, parents are not involved in a general parent-education program but are offered an opportunity to learn techniques for helping their children to succeed in school. The contract offered to participating mothers is believed to be honest in that there is little chance that the parents will fail to see positive change because it has been shown that their children do have a better chance for school success.

Home-based intervention programs must also deal with the major ethical issues brought about by their invasion of the privacy of the home and exertion of pressure on parents to change their mode of interaction with their children. In considering the ethics involved in penetrating into the home, it is important to weigh the possible dangers in terms of what the program offers in return. From a simplistic point of view, it may be said that the invasion-of-privacy question does not pertain to HIPPY since participation in the program is voluntary. A more realistic approach, however, would take into account the fact that a promise is offered through participation and that this promise is an important factor in the mother's decision to participate. Mothers of disadvantaged children in Israel suffer anxiety due to their children's poor school achievement because they clearly feel that success in school will lead to success in society and will help their children move into the mainstream (which they would have liked to have done themselves). Because HIPPY offers hope in this area, it is probable that although the program requirements are clearly outlined ahead of time, mothers join without considering the degree to which they and their homes will be affected. They are unable to anticipate either the impact of the aide's regular visits or the pressures to meet the program's requirements.

Both of these factors may be manipulatory, with all the negative connotations involved. And the fact that modern social mores accept that manipulation is inherent in all educational activity does not negate the fact that an ethical problem exists. All that can be said is that any program that sets out to change something about the behavior of its participants is, by its very nature, manipulatory. The issue of manipulation in educational programs, however, must be viewed in terms of the extent to which the manipulatory process can be expected to produce the desired results. The honesty of the contract offered mothers who join HIPPY is a prime factor in weighing the ethical considerations of home-based intervention.

HIPPY endeavors to guard against untoward manipulation by allowing mothers to drop out of the program at any time during the first year; by giving them another opportunity to decide whether they wish to continue at the beginning of the second and third years, after they have full knowledge of what is entailed; and by a structure that affords them an opportunity to air their grievances and that provides an open forum for them to discuss questions troubling them.

A more crucial question in this context, and one that is more difficult to answer, is the extent to which the values and expectations represented by the HIPPY model are congruent with those of the participating families. If they are not, how confident can one be that what is being offered is better, and can one justify the conflicts that the participants may have to face in their attempts to deal with values and expectations that differ from their own?

The question is difficult because it has no absolute answer. HIPPY represents a set of values believed to be closer to the educational establishment than those of its clients; as such they can be expected to be generally acceptable and desirable. Mothers who participate in HIPPY do so with the idea of producing change in their children that will enable them to join the mainstream. It may also be suggested that although the values and expectations of the program planners may not be identical with those of the mothers, they are close enough to preclude serious conflicts and negative reactions.

Many of the issues relating to the expansion of educational programs in general have already been faced by HIPPY. As the program increases in size, decisions must be taken as to the direction in which it will grow. For example, the question arises as to what extent HIPPY will attempt to reach that portion of the target population that needs the program but does not want it. A corollary question is the extent to which we should consider requests to set up programs for those who want it but cannot be considered to need it. If the decision is made to reach out to one or both of these groups, adjustments will have to be made in the program to meet their needs. The supervisory and administrative staffs will grow with age and growth in numbers. And in order to avoid becoming involved in a cumbersome administrative structure, there will have to be experimentation with various methods of releasing administrative control over local programs that are well established. It is hoped that this can be accomplished without diminishing the quality of these programs.

Finally, a decision will have to be taken as to how large HIPPY should become. It may be that since Israel is a small country, a point of natural saturation will be reached and that further growth in HIPPY will cease when that point has been reached. But if new populations are to be included from time to time, such a saturation point will be delayed. From the viewpoint of good program planning, it would seem expedient to determine the broadest potential population, whatever that may turn out to be, and to expand until that population is being fully served. HIPPY will reach a point of balance and stability whereby it will be accepting new (and younger) families as it finishes serving older families that are no longer child bearing. If the trend toward smaller families continues, there will be a natural diminishing of the number of participating families. Optimistically there will be a further diminishing of numbers as the population of disadvantaged children grows smaller, due in part to programs such as HIPPY.

Bibliography

Adiel, S. 1970. "Asor lemifalei tipuah ochlusiat ha-talmidim bevatei ha-sefer." In S. Adiel, ed., [A decade of enrichment programs for the population of pupils in school]. Jerusalem: Ministry of Education and Culture.

Alon, E. 1980. "Self-Concept Changes in Adult Participants of the Home Instruction Program for Preschool Youngsters." Master's thesis, Hebrew University of Jerusalem.

Barbrack, C.R., and Horton, D.M. 1970. "Educational Intervention in the Home and Paraprofessional Career Development: A First Generation Mother Study." ERIC Document Reproduction Service No. ED 045 190. Nashville, Tenn.: George Peabody College for Teachers.

Barletta, C.; Boger, R.; Lezotte, L.; and Hull, B., eds. 1978 *Planning and Implementing Parent/Community Involvement into the Instructional Delivery System.* Proceedings from a Parent/Community Involvement Conference, Midwest Teacher Corps Network, East Lansing, Michigan.

Barton, K.; Dielman, T.E.; and Cattell, R.B. 1974. "Child Rearing Practices and Achievement in School." *Journal of Genetic Psychology* 124:155-165.

Bayley, N., and Schaefer, E.S. 1960. "Relationships between Socioeconomic Variables and the Behavior of Mothers toward Young Children." *Journal of Genetic Psychology* 96:61-77.

Bee, H.L.; Van Egeren, L.; Streissguth, A.B.; Nyman, B.A.; and Leckie, M.S. 1969. "Social Class Differences in Maternal Teaching Strategies and Speech Patterns." *Developmental Psychology* 1:726-734.

Berman, P., and McLaughlin, M.W. 1978. *Federal Programs Supporting Educational Change. Vol. 8: Implementing and Sustaining Innovations.* R-1589/8-HEW. Prepared for the U.S. Office of Education, Department of Health, Education and Welfare. Santa Monica, Calif.: Rand Corporation, May.

Bernstein, B. 1961. "Social Structure, Language, and Learning." *Education Research* 3(3):163-176.

Bielecky, F., and Egozi, M. 1978. *Statistical Data on the Education System.* Jerusalem: Ministry of Education and Culture.

Boehm, A.E. 1967. *Boehm Test of Basic Concepts Manual.* New York: Psychological Corporation.

Bronfenbrenner, U. 1969. "The Social Side of Socialization." Address delivered at the Hebrew University of Jerusalem, January.

_____. 1974. "Is Early Intervention Effective?" *Day Care and Early Education* 2 (2):14-18, 44.

Brophy, J.E. 1970. "Mothers as Teachers of Their Own Preschool Children: The Influence of Socioeconomic Status and Task Structure on Teaching Specificity." *Child Development* 41(1):79-94.

Bruner, J.S.; Goodnow, J.J.; and Austin, G.A. 1956. *A Study of Thinking.* New York: Wiley.

Carroll, J. 1964. *Language and Thought.* Englewood Cliffs, N.J.: Prentice-Hall.

Clark, B.R. 1962. *Educating the Expert Society.* San Francisco: Chandler Publishing Co.

Clarke-Stewart, K.A., with Apfel, N. 1979. "Evaluating Parental Effects on Child Development." In L.S. Shulman, ed., *Review of Research in Education.* Itasca, Ill.: F.E. Peacock.

Cohen, H. 1980. "Tochnit ha-etgar: teur halachah lemaaseh unituah hama' arachot." [HIPPY: Description and analysis of processes in its operation] Mimeographed. Jerusalem: National Council of Jewish Women Research Institute for Innovation in Education, Hebrew University.

Coleman, J.S.; Campbell, E.Q.; Hobson, C.J.; McPartland, J.; Mood, A.M.; Weinfield, F.D.; and York, R.L. 1966. *Equality of Educational Opportunity.* U.S. Office of Health, Education and Welfare, Office of Education. Washington, D.C.: U.S. Government Printing Office.

Cremin, L.A. 1974. "The Family as Educator: Some Comments on the Recent Historiography." In H.J. Leichter, ed., *The Family as Educator.* New York: Teachers College Press.

Davis, D., and Kugelmass, J. 1974. "Home Environment: The Impact of the Home Instruction Program for Preschool Youngsters (HIPPY) on the Mother's Role as an Educator. An Interim Evaluation." Mimeographed. Jerusalem: National Council of Jewish Women Research Institute for Innovation in Education, Hebrew University.

Eisenstadt, S.N. 1955. *The Absorption of Immigrants.* Glencoe, Ill.: Free Press.

_____. 1956. "Traditional and Modern Social Values and Economic Development." *Annals of the American Academy of Political and Social Sciences* (May):145-156.

Elkind, D.; Van Doorninck, W.; and Schwarz, C. 1967. "Perceptual Activity and Concept Attainment." *Child Development* 38(4):1153-1161.

Feshbach, N.D. 1973. "Cross-cultural Studies of Teaching Styles in Four-Year-Olds and Their Mothers." In A.D. Pick, ed., *Minnesota Symposia on Child Psychology.* Vol. 7. Minneapolis: University of Minnesota Press.

Fitts, W.H. 1965. *Manual for the Tennessee Self-Concept Scale.* Nashville, Tenn.: Counselor REcordings and Tests.

Frankel, Y. 1976. *Adaptation of Tennessee Self-Concept Scale.* Ramat Gan: Bar Ilan University.

Frostig, M., and Horne, D. 1964. *The Frostig Program for the Development of Visual Perception.* Chicago: Follett Publishing Company.

Frostig, M.; Maslow, P.; Lefever, D.W.; and Whittlesey, J.R.B. 1961. "A Developmental Test of Visual Perception for Evaluating Normal and Neurologically Handicapped Children." *Perceptual and Motor Skills* 12:383-394.

Garber, M., and Ware, W. 1972. "The Home Environment as a Predictor of School Achievement." *Theory into Practice* 11(3):190-196.

Getzels, J.W. 1974. "Socialization and Education: A Note on Discontinuities." In H.J. Leichter, ed., *The Family as Educator.* New York: Teachers College Press.

Goldberg, R.J. 1978. "Development in the Family and School Context: Who Is Responsible for the Education of Young Children in America?" Paper presented at the National Association for the Education of Young Children Annual Conference, New York, N.Y., August 17-20.

Goldhaber, D. 1979. "Does the Changing View of Early Experience Imply a Changing View of Early Development?" In L.G. Katz, ed., *Current Topics in Early Childhood Education,* Vol. 2. Norwood, N.J.: Ablex Publishing Corporation.

Gordon, I.J., and Breivogel, W.F. 1976. *Building Effective Home-School Relationships.* Boston, Mass.: Allyn & Bacon.

Gordon, I.J.; Guinagh, B.; and Jester, R.E. 1977. "The Florida Parent Education Infant and Toddler Programs." In M.C. Day and R.K. Parker, eds., *The Preschool in Action.* Boston, Mass.: Allyn & Bacon.

Gotkin, L.G. 1963. "Cognitive Development and the Issue of Individual Differences." *Programmed Instruction* 3(1).

_____. 1968. *Programmed Instruction as a Strategy for Developing Curricula for Disadvantaged Children.* Monographs of the Society for Research in Child Development 33 (B, Serial No. 124).

Gross, M.B. 1970. "Preschool Prediction of Academic Achievement." *Psychological Reports* 26(1):278.

Gupta, W. 1967. "Echoic Responding in Disadvantaged Preschool Children: Drill vs. Story Telling." Paper presented at the meeting of the California Educational Research Association, Los Angeles, March.

Hess, R.D., and Shipman, V.C. 1965. "Early Blocks to Children's Learning." *Children* 12(5):185-195.

_____. 1968. "Early Experience and the Socialization of Cognitive Modes in Children." In R.G. Kuhler, ed., *Studies in Educational Psychology.* Waltham, Mass: Blaisdell Publishing Co.

Hively, W. 1962. "Programming Stimuli in Matching to Sample." *Journal of the Experimental Analysis of Behavior* 5:279-298.

Hunt, J. McV. 1964. "The Psychological Basis for Using Preschool Enrichment as an Antidote for Cultural Deprivation." *Merrill-Palmer Quarterly of Behavior and Development* 10(3):209-248.

Inbar, M., and Adler, C. 1977. *Ethnic Integration in Israel.* New Brunswick, N.J.: Transaction Books.

Jencks, C.; Smith, M.; Acland, H.; Bane, M.J.; Cohen, D.; Gintis, H.; Heyns, B.; and Michelson, S. 1973. *Inequality: A Reassessment of the Effect of Family and Schooling in America.* New York: Harper & Row.

Jensen, A.R. 1962. "Learning in the Preschool Years." *Journal of Nursery Education* 18:133-139.

Jester, R.E. 1969. "Focus on Parent Education as a Means of Altering the Child's Environment." ERIC Document Reproduction Service No. ED 033 758. Gainesville, Fla.: Gainesville Institute for Development of Human Resources, Florida University.

John, V.P. 1964. "A Brief Survey of Research on the Characteristics of Children from Low-Income Backgrounds." Prepared for the U.S. Commissioner on Education, August.

Jones, P.A. 1972. "Home Environment and the Development of Verbal Ability." *Child Development* 43:1081-1086.

Kafner, F.H. 1973. "Behavior Modification—An Overview." In C.E. Thorensen, ed., *Behavior Modification in Education.* Chicago: University of Chicago Press.

Kariv, Y., and Silberstein, P. 1977a. "Doch al ha-ra'ayonot shene'erchu im gannenot shel yeladim shehishtatefu shana be-tochnit ha-etgar." [Report on interviews with kindergarten teachers of children who participated for one year in the HIPPY program] Mimeographed. Jerusalem: National Council of Jewish Women Research Institute for Innovation in Education, Hebrew University, August.

——. 1977b. "Ha-ma'akav aharei ha-hesegim ha-chinuchiim shel proyekt ha-etgar. Doch mispar 1. Ifiunum basisiim shel ha-ahayyim ha-bogerim." [Follow-up of educational achievements in the HIPPY project. Report No. 1. Basic characteristics of older siblings] Mimeographed. Jerusalem: National Council of Jewish Women Research Institute for Innovation in Education, Hebrew University.

——. 1978a. "Ha-ma'akav aharei ha-hesegim shel proyekt ha-etgar. Doch benaim mispar 2. Ifiunim basisiim legabei kol ochlusiat ha-mehkar be-mivhanei ha-hesegim be-ivrit uveheshbon vehitnahagut bakita—ulgabay kvutza nivheret be-yetzirat musagim. [Follow-up of achievements in the HIPPY project. Interim report No. 2. Basic characteristics of the total research population in achievement tests in Hebrew, mathematics, and classroom behavior—and for a selected group in creation of concepts] Mimeographed. Jerusalem: National Council of Jewish Women Research Institute for Innovation in Education, Hebrew University.

_____. 1978b. "Ha-ma'akav aha'rei ha-hesegim shel proyekt ha-etgar. Doch benaim mispar 3." [Follow-up of achievements in the HIPPY project. Interim report No.3] Mimeographed. Jerusalem: National Council of Jewish Women Research Institute for Innovation in Education, Hebrew University.

Karnes, M.B.; Teska, J.A.; and Hodgins, A.S. 1970a. "The Effect of Four Programs of Classroom Intervention on the Intellectual and Language Development of 4 Year Old Disadvantaged Children." *American Journal of Orthopsychiatry* 40(1):58-76.

Karnes, M.M.: Teska, J.A.; Hodgins, A.S.; and Badger, E.D. 1970b. "Educational Intervention at Home by Mothers of Disadvantaged Infants." *Child Development* 41:925-935.

Karnes, M.E., et al. 1978 "Immediate, Short-Term and Long-Range Effects of Five Preschool Programs for Disadvantaged Children." ERIC Document Reproduction Service No. ED 152 043. March.

Kendler, T.S. 1963. "Development of Mediating Responses in Children." In J.C. Wright and J. Kagan, eds., *Basic Cognitive Processes in Children,* pp. 33-48. Monographs of the Society for Research in Child Development, 28 (2, Serial No. 86).

Keisler, E.R., and McNeil, J.D. 1961. "Teaching Scientific Theory to First Grade Pupils by Auto-Instructional Device." *Harvard Educational Review* 31(1):73-83.

Landa, E.R. 1979. Foreword to H.A. Green and J. Cohen, *Research in Action.* Jerusalem: Hebrew University.

Lazar, I.; Hubbell, V.R.; and Murray, H. 1977. *Summary Report: The Persistence of Preschool Effects. A Long-Term Follow-up of Fourteen Infant and Preschool Experiments.* DHEW Publication No. (OHDS) 78-30129. Washington, D.C.: U.S. Government Printing Office.

Lightfoot, S.L. 1978. *Worlds Apart.* New York: Basic Books.

Lombard, A.D. 1968. "Effectiveness of Instruction in Puzzle Assembly Skills with Preschool Children." Ph.D. dissertation, University of California, Los Angeles.

_____. 1973. "Home Instruction Program for Preschool Youngsters (HIPPY)." Final Report. Mimeographed. Jerusalem: National Council of Jewish Women Research Institute for Innovation in Education, Hebrew University.

Luria, A.R. 1961. *"The Role of Speech in the Regulation of Normal and Abnormal Behavior.* London: Pergamon Press.

Lynn, R. 1963. "Reading Readiness and the Perceptual Abilities of Young Children." *Educational Research* 6(1):10-15.

Madden, J.; Levenstein, P.; and Levenstein, S. 1976. "Longitudinal I.Q. Outcomes of the Mother-Child Home Program." Child Development 47(4):1015-1025.

Merrifield, P.R.; Guilford, J.P.; Christensen, P.R.; and Frick, J.W. 1960. *A Factor-Analytic Study of Problem-Solving Abilities.* Los Angeles: University of Southern California, Psychological Laboratory, March.

Micotti, A.R. 1970. *Dame School Project (Bilingual Preschool Project) Final Report.* San Jose, Calif.: Santa Clara County Office of Education, August.

Minkovich, A.; Davis D.; and Bashi, J. 1977. *An Evaluation Study of Israeli Elementary Schools.* Jerusalem: Hebrew University.

O'Keefe, R.A. 1979. "What Head Start Means to Families." In L.G. Katz, ed., *Current Topics in Early Childhood Education,* Vol. 2. Norwood, N.J.: Ablex Publishing Corporation.

Olmsted, P., and Jester, E. 1972. "Mother-Child Interaction in a Teaching Situation." *Theory into Practice* 11(3):163-171.

Ortar, G., and Ben-Shachar, N. 1972. *Mivchanei havanat hanikra bechinuch ha-yesodi (9).* [Tests in reading comprehension in elementary education (Series 9)] Jerusalem: Ministry of Education and Culture, January.

Passow, A.H., and Elliott, D.P. 1968. "The Nature and Needs of the Educationally Disadvantaged." In A.H. Passow, ed., *Developing Programs for the Educationally Disadvantaged.* New York: Teachers College Press.

Paynton, N. 1972. "Mother-Child Verbal Communication: The Relationship between Mother's Question-Asking Behavior and Child's Response." Master's thesis, Hebrew University of Jerusalem.

Piaget, J. 1967. *The Language and Thought of the Child.* London: Routledge and Kegan Paul.

Plowden, B. 1967. *Children and their Primary Schools.* Report of the Central Advisory Council for Education (England). London: Her Majesty's Stationery Office.

Radin, N. 1974. "Observed Maternal Behavior with Four-Year-Old Boys and Girls in Lower-Class Families." *Child Development* 45:1126-1131.

Riessman, F. 1966. *Helping the Disadvantaged Pupil to Learn More Easily.* Englewood Cliffs, N.J.: Prentice-Hall.

_____. 1972. "Education of the Culturally Deprived Child." In W.J. Gnagey, P.A. Chesebro, and J.J. Johnson, eds., *Learning Environments: Readings in Educational Psychology.* New York: Holt, Rinehart & Winston.

Rinot, M. 1971. *Hevrat ha-ezra leyehudei Germania be-yetzira uvema'avak.* [The assistance association for German Jews in creation and in struggle] Jerusalem: Hebrew University Ministry of Education and Culture; Haifa: University of Haifa; Leo Baeck College.

Shamgar-Handelman, L., and Belkin, R. 1979. "Family Functioning and Children's Achievements in School." Mimeographed. Jerusalem: National Council of Jewish Women Research Institute for Innovation in Education, Hebrew University.

Shuval, J. 1963. *Immigrants on the Threshold.* New York: Atherton Press.

Silberstein, P. 1979. "Ma'akav aharei hesegei yeladim be-proyekt ha-etgar. Doch benaim mispar 4." [Follow-up of children's achievements in the HIPPY project. Interim report no. 4] Mimeographed. Jerusalem: National Council of Jewish Women Research Institute for Innovation in Education, Hebrew University.

Smooha, S. 1978. *Israel: Pluralism and Conflict.* London: Routledge & Kegan Paul.

Spilerman, S., and Habib, J. 1976." Development Towns in Israel: The Role of Community in Creating Ethnic Disparities in Labor Force Characteristics." *American Journal of Sociology* 81(4):781-812.

Sulzer, B., and Mayer, G.R. 1972. *Behavior Modification Procedures for School Personnel.* Hinsdale, Ill.: Dryden Press.

Swan, R., and Stavros, H. 1973. "Child Rearing Practices Associated with the Development of Cognitive Skills in Children of Low Socioeconomic Areas." *Early Child Development and Care* 2:23-28.

Van De Riet, V.; Van De Riet, H.; and Sprigle, H. 1968-1969. "The Effectiveness of a New Sequential Learning Program with Culturally Disadvantaged Preschool Children." *Journal of School Psychology* 7(3):5-15.

Vopava, J., and Royce, J. 1978. "Comparison of the Long Term Effects of Infant and Preschool Programs on Academic Performances." ERIC Document Reproduction Service No. ED 152 428. Ithaca, N.Y.: Cornell University.

Vygotsky, L.S. 1962. *Thought and Language.* Translated and edited by E. Hanfmann and G. Vakar. Cambridge, Mass.: M.I.T. Press.

Weikart, D.P., and Schweinhart, L. 1979. "Preliminary Findings on the Social and Economic Adjustment of Young Adults Who Completed the Experimental Preschool." Paper presented at the annual meeting of the American Educational Research Association, San Francisco, April 8-12.

Westinghouse Learning Corporation and Ohio State University. 1969. *The Impact of Head Start: An Evaluation of the Effects of Head Start on Children's Cognitive and Affective Development.* Springfield, Va.: Clearinghouse for Federal Scientific and Technical Information.

Winer, B.J. 1962. *Statistical Principles in Experimental Design.* New York: McGraw-Hill.

Zigler, E. 1978. "The Effectiveness of Head Start: Another Look." *Educational Psychologist* 13(1):71-77.

Appendix A
Examples of Workbook
Activities for
Four Year Olds

Week: C - 1
Activity: <u>Loud sound - soft sound (1)</u>

Work Page (1)

1. (Materials: A radio)
   (Turn on the radio).

2. (Ask) DO YOU HEAR SOUNDS?
                                      - Yes.

---

3. (Turn off the radio).

   DO YOU HEAR SOUNDS NOW?

                        -No.

4. (Say)

   NOW I DO NOT HEAR SOUNDS.
   SWITCH ON THE RADIO AND
   I WILL HEAR THEM.

---

5. (Turn up the volume to very high).

   (Say): THAT IS A LOUD SOUND.
          SAY AFTER ME:
          THAT IS A LOUD SOUND.
          -That is a loud sound.

6. (Turn down the volume to very low).

   (Say): THAT IS A SOFT SOUND.
          SAY AFTER ME:
          THAT IS A SOFT SOUND.
           - That is a soft sound.

---

7. (Say to the child)

   TURN UP THE RADIO TO A LOUD SOUND.
   WHAT SOUND IS THAT?
   - That is a loud sound.

8. (Say):

   NOW MAKE A VERY SOFT SOUND.
   WHAT SOUND IS THAT?
   -That is a soft sound.

"HIPPY" - Age 4 (1979)

Week: C - 1
Activity: <u>Loud sound - soft sound (1)</u>

Work page (2)

9. (Turn the knob to very high volume)
 	
   THAT IS A VERY LOUD SOUND.
   IT IS NOT PLEASANT TO LISTEN TO.
	10.(Turn to a <u>very soft</u> sound)
	
	   THAT IS A VERY SOFT SOUND.
	   THAT ISN'T PLEASANT TO LISTEN TO
	   EITHER.

11. (Turn to a medium volume).

   THAT'S A PLEASANT SOUND TO LISTEN TO.
   WHAT KIND OF SOUND IS THAT?
   - That's a pleasant sound.

---

12. (Say): I'LL TELL YOU HOW TO TURN THE KNOB
            AND YOU TURN IT.

TURN IT UP TO A VERY LOUD SOUND
TURN IT DOWN TO A VERY SOFT SOUND
MAKE IT LOUDER AGAIN
MAKE IT SO THAT IT'S A PLEASANT SOUND
TURN IT DOWN TO A SOFT SOUND
TURN IT UP TO A LOUD SOUND

---

13. NOW CLOSE YOUR EYES AND LISTEN.

  (Turn to a loud sound): WHAT SOUND DO YOU HEAR?
                    -A loud sound.

  (Turn to a soft sound): WHAT SOUND DO YOU HEAR?
                    -A soft sound.

  (Adjust to a pleasant sound):WHAT SOUND DO Y U HEAR?
                    -A pleasant sound.

  (Turn up to a very loud sound): WHAT SOUND IS THIS?
                    - A very loud sound.

  (Turn down to a very sot sound):WHAT SOUND IS THIS?
                    - A very soft sound.

"HIPPY" - Age 4 (1979)

Week: C - 2
Activity: Small-big (8)

Work Page (1)

1. MARK THE SMALLEST	2. MARK THE BIGGEST
A. (Example):	A. (Example):
B.	B.
C.	C.
D.	D.
E.	E.
F.	F.
G.	G.

"HIPPY" Age 4 (1975)

Week: C - 2
ACTIVITY: Same-different (8)

Work page (3)

1. ARE THE PICTURES THE SAME OR DIFFERENT? - The pictures are the same.

2. MARK THE TWO PICTURES WITH X IN THE SAME COLOR (for example, red).

1. ARE THE PICTURES THE SAME OR DIFFERENT? - The pictures are different.

2. MARK THE TWO PICTURES WITH X IN DIFFERENT COLORS.

1. ARE THE PICTURES THE SAME OR DIFFERENT? - The pictures are the same.

2. MARK THE TWO PICTURES WITH X IN THE SAME COLOR.

"HIPPY" Age 4 (1975)

Week: C - 5
Activity: <u>Shapes and colors (4)</u>

Work page (1)

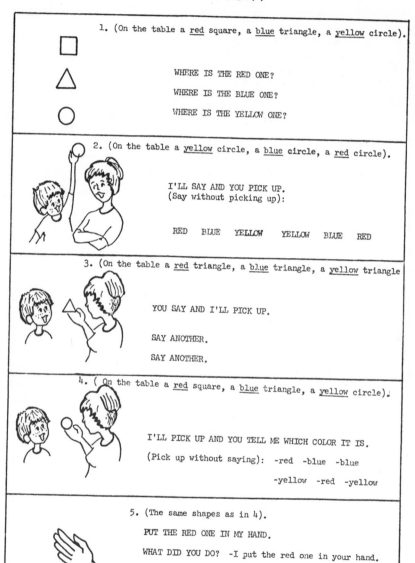

1. (On the table a <u>red</u> square, a <u>blue</u> triangle, a <u>yellow</u> circle).

WHERE IS THE RED ONE?

WHERE IS THE BLUE ONE?

WHERE IS THE YELLOW ONE?

2. (On the table a <u>yellow</u> circle, a <u>blue</u> circle, a <u>red</u> circle).

I'LL SAY AND YOU PICK UP.
(Say without picking up):

RED   BLUE   YELLOW   YELLOW   BLUE   RED

3. (On the table a <u>red</u> triangle, a <u>blue</u> triangle, a <u>yellow</u> triangle

YOU SAY AND I'LL PICK UP.

SAY ANOTHER.

SAY ANOTHER.

4. (On the table a <u>red</u> square, a <u>blue</u> triangle, a <u>yellow</u> circle).

I'LL PICK UP AND YOU TELL ME WHICH COLOR IT IS.

(Pick up without saying): -red -blue -blue
                                          -yellow -red -yellow

5. (The same shapes as in 4).

PUT THE RED ONE IN MY HAND.

WHAT DID YOU DO? -I put the red one in your hand.

PUT THE BLUE ONE IN MY HAND.

WHAT DID YOU DO? -I put the blue one in your hand.

"HIPPY" - Age 4 (1979)

Week: C - 5
Activity: <u>Shapes and colors (4)</u>

Work page (2)

---

1. (Materials: red square, blue triangle, yellow circle).

PUT THE YELLOW ONE ON THE TABLE.

WHAT DID YOU DO? -I put the yellow one on the table.

---

2. (Materials: the same shapes)

PUT THE YELLOW ONE ON THE RED ONE.

WHAT DID YOU DO? -I put the yellow one on the red one.

---

3. (Materials: the same shapes)

PUT THE RED ONE ON THE BLUE ONE.

WHAT DID YOU DO? -I put the red one on the blue one.

---

4. (Materials: the same shapes)

PUT THE BLUE ONE ON THE YELLOW ONE.

WHAT DID YOU DO? -I put the blue one on the yellow one.

---

5. NOW YOU TELL ME WHERE TO PUT THE RED ONE.

   NOW YOU TELL ME WHERE TO PUT THE BLUE ONE.

   NOW YOU TELL ME WHERE TO PUT THE YELLOW ONE.

"HIPPY" - Age 4 (1979)

Appendix B
Examples of Workbook
Activities for
Five Year Olds

Week: C – 4
Activity: What do they do? (8)

Work page (1)

1. (Open the book "What Do They Do" at page 14).

   (Point to the tools and ask):

   WHAT ARE ALL THESE? – They are the tools of the man who repairs the tires.

2. WHAT IS THE MAN HOLDING IN HIS HAND? – A tire.

3. THERE IS A PUNCTURE IN THE TIRE AND THE MAN WANTS TO REPAIR IT.

   WHERE WILL HE PUT THE TIRE WHEN IT IS REPAIRED? – He will attach it to the truck.

4. WHAT DOES THE MAN NEED THE TOOLS FOR? – Those are his tools for repairing tires.

5. A MAN WHO REPAIRS CARS AND TRUCKS IS CALLED A MECHANIC. SAY AFTER ME: MECHANIC – Mechanic

(Turn to page 17 and say):

6. LOOK AT THE PICTURE AND TELL ME WHAT CLOTHES THE GIRL IS WEARING. – The girl is wearing a white apron and a nurse's cap.

7. HOW DO WE KNOW THAT SHE IS A NURSE? – Because of the clothes she is wearing.

8. WHAT DO WE CALL A NURSE'S CLOTHES? – A nurse's uniform.

9. DO YOU SEE WHO IS SICK IN THE PICTURE? – The girl's doll is sick.

10. HOW DO YOU KNOW THAT SHE IS SICK? – She is lying in bed because she is sick.

11. WHAT IS THE NURSE GIVING TO THE SICK DOLL? – She is giving her medicine and looking after her.

"HIPPY" – Age 5 (1979)

Week: C - 4
Activity: What do they do? (8)

Work page (2)

12. (Point to the picture on page 16 and ask):
    WHY IS THE BOY LYING IN BED? - Because he is sick.

13. WHO IS SITTING ON THE CHAIR? - The doctor.

14. WHAT IS HE DOING TO THE PATIENT? - He is taking his temperature.

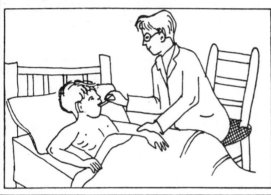

14. THE DOCTOR
    EXAMINES THE
    PATIENT.

    WHAT WILL HE
    GIVE HIM?
    - He will give
    him medicine
    to make him
    better.

(Turn to page 18 and ask):

15. WHAT DOES THE MAN HAVE IN HIS HAND?
    - He has a hammer.

16. WHAT IS THE MAN DOING WITH THE
    HAMMER? - He is taking nails out of
    the board.

17. WHAT WILL THE MAN DO WITH THE BOARDS?
    - He will make furniture with the
    boards.

18. WHAT DO WE CALL A MAN WHO WORKS WITH
    BOARDS AND MAKES FURNITURE? - We call
    him a carpenter.

19. WHAT IS THE CARPENTER WEARING? - The
    carpenter is wearing overalls and a
    shirt.

20. THOSE ARE HIS WORK CLOTHES.
    REPEAT AFTER ME: THOSE ARE WORK
    CLOTHES. - Those are work clothes.

"HIPPY" - Age 5 (1979)

Week: C – 4
Activity: Matrix (36)

Work page (1)

1. HERE IS A PICTURE OF A CAT. WHO IS STROKING IT? – A man.

5. HERE IS ANOTHER PICTURE OF A CAT. WHO IS STROKING IT? – A girl.

9. HERE IS ANOTHER PICTURE OF A CAT. WHO IS STROKING IT? – A boy.

2. WHO IS THAT? – That is a man. WHAT IS HE DOING? – He is feeding the bird.

6. WHO IS FEEDING THIS BIRD? – The girl.

10. HERE IS A PICTURE OF A BIRD. WHO IS FEEDING IT? –The boy.

3. AND WHAT IS THIS MAN DOING? – He is holding on to the dog.

7. AND WHO IS HOLDING ON TO THIS DOG? – The girl.

11. AND HERE IS A PICTURE OF A DOG. WHO IS HOLDING ON TO IT? – The boy.

4. SO THEN, SHOW ME THE ROW OF MEN.

8. SHOW ME THE ROW OF GIRLS.

12. WHO APPEARS ON ALL OF THE PICTURES IN THIS ROW? – Boys.

"HIPPY" – Age 5 (1979)

Week: C - 5   Activity: Matrix (37)   Work page (1)

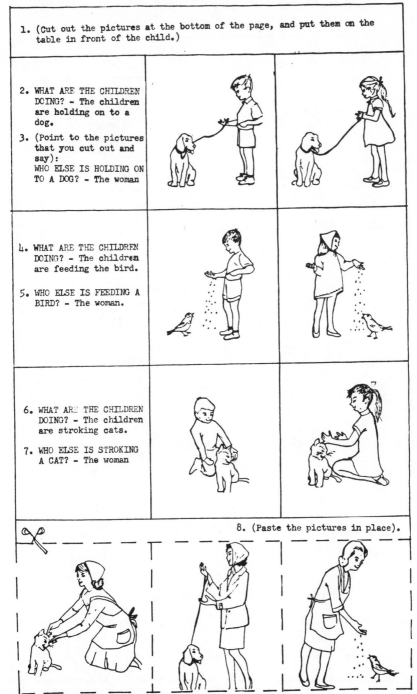

1. (Cut out the pictures at the bottom of the page, and put them on the table in front of the child.)

2. WHAT ARE THE CHILDREN DOING? - The children are holding on to a dog.

3. (Point to the pictures that you cut out and say):
WHO ELSE IS HOLDING ON TO A DOG? - The woman

4. WHAT ARE THE CHILDREN DOING? - The children are feeding the bird.

5. WHO ELSE IS FEEDING A BIRD? - The woman.

6. WHAT ARE THE CHILDREN DOING? - The children are stroking cats.

7. WHO ELSE IS STROKING A CAT? - The woman

8. (Paste the pictures in place).

"HIPPY" - Age 5 (1979

Week: C - 5
Activity: Connecting same pictures (8)

Work page (1)

1. (Point to row 1 and say):
   IN THIS ROW ALL THINGS WHICH ARE THE SAME
   HAVE THE SAME MARK.

2. (Point to the big squares and say):
   THESE PICTURES ARE MARKED WITH AN X
   BECAUSE THEY ARE THE SAME. WHY ARE THEY
   THE SAME? - In all of them there is a
   big square.

3. (Point to the small squares):
   THESE PICTURES ARE MARKED WITH A CIRCLE
   BECAUSE THEY ARE THE SAME. WHY ARE
   THEY THE SAME? - In all of them there
   is a small square.

4. GO OVER THE MARKS WITH A PENCIL.

5. (Go over row 2 and say):

   A. SHOW ME THE PICTURES THAT ARE THE SAME.
      WHY ARE THEY THE SAME? - In all of them the triangle is
                             on its side / upright.
                             (Match your response to the
      MARK THEM WITH AN X.   picture the child points to).

   B. SHOW ME THE OTHER PICTURES THAT ARE THE SAME.
      WHY ARE THEY THE SAME? - In all of them the triangle is
                             on its side/upright
                             (answer according to the child's
                             choice).

6. (Continue with the same questions for row 3).

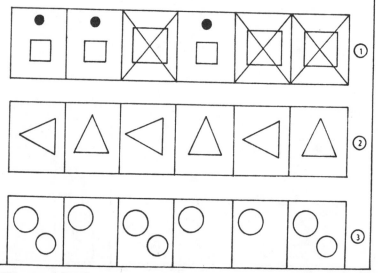

"HIPPY" - Age 5 (1979)

Appendix B

Week: C - 5
Activity: Connecting same pictures (8)

Work page (2)

(Go row by row, in order, and for each row say):

1. SHOW ME THE PICTURES THAT ARE THE SAME.
   WHY ARE THEY THE SAME? -(Child answers)
   MARK THEM WITH AN X.

2. SHOW ME THE OTHER PICTURES THAT ARE THE SAME.
   WHY ARE THEY THE SAME? -(child answers)
   MARK THEM WITH A CIRCLE.

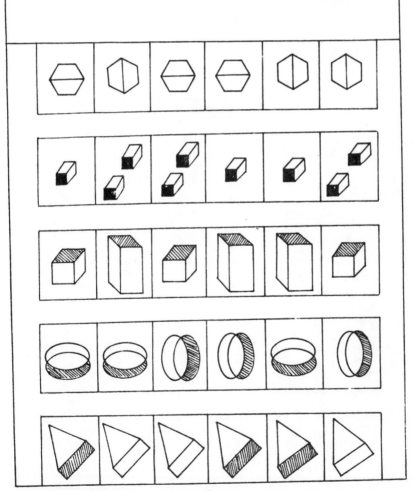

"HIPPY" - Age 5 (1979) - 19 -

Appendix C
Examples of Workbook
Activities for
Six Year Olds

Week: C
Activity: Fill in what is missing (3)

Work Page (1)

1. SHOW ME A CHAIR WHICH HAS SOMETHING MISSING.
   FILL IN WHAT IS MISSING.

2. ARE THE TWO CHAIRS COMPLETE NOW? - Yes.

1. SHOW ME A LADDER WHICH HAS SOMETHING MISSING.
   FILL IN WHAT IS MISSING.

2. ARE THE TWO LADDERS COMPLETE NOW? - Yes.

"HIPPY" - Age 6 (1979)

Week: C
Activity: Fill in what is missing (3)

Work page (2)

1. SHOW ME A GLASS WHICH HAS SOMETHING MISSING.
   FILL IN WHAT IS MISSING.

2. ARE THE TWO GLASSES COMPLETE NOW? - Yes.

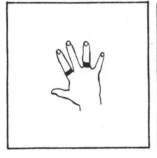 

1. SHOW ME A HAND WITH SOMETHING MISSSING.
   FILL IN WHAT IS MISSING.

2. ARE THE TWO HANDS THE SAME NOW? - Yes.

Week: C
Activity: Outlines (3)

Work page (1)

(Materials: crayons - red, blue, yellow, green).

1. (Put this page on the table in front of both of you and say):

I WILL TELL YOU WHICH SHAPE TO MARK AND YOU MARK IT.

WHICH IS THE SHAPE OF THE SHOE?	MARK IT IN RED.
WHICH IS THE SHAPE OF THE HAND?	MARK IT IN BLUE.
WHICH IS THE SHAPE OF THE PENCIL?	MARK IT IN YELLOW.
WHICH IS THE SHAPE OF THE SPOON?	MARK IT IN GREEN.
WHICH IS THE SHAPE OF THE QUARTER?	MARK IT IN BLUE.
WHICH IS THE SHAPE OF THE DIME?	MARK IT IN YELLOW.
WHICH IS THE SHAPE OF THE FOOT?	MARK IT IN GREEN.
WHICH IS THE SHAPE OF THE BOTTLE CAP?	MARK IT IN RED.

2. NOW YOU ASK ME AND I'LL POINT TO THE SHAPE.
   ASK ME. (If the child finds it difficult, say to him):
          TELL ME WHERE IS THE SHAPE OF THE SHOE? (etc.)
   ASK ME AGAIN.
   AND AGAIN.
   AND AGAIN.

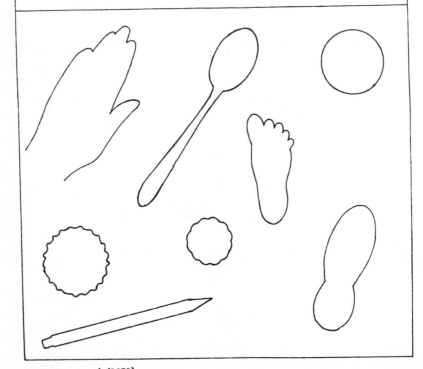

"HIPPY" - Age 6 (1979)

Week: C
Activity: Outlines (3)

Work page (2)

1. (Say):
   CUT OUT THE PICTURES OF THE FRUIT ALONG THE BLACK LINE.

   PUT THE FRUIT HERE (point) AND OUTLINE THEM IN BLUE.

   (If the child finds it difficult, show him how to do
   one fruit, and let him continue on his own with the
   remaining fruits).

2. CUT OUT THE PICTURES OF THE DIFFERENT KINDS OF
   TRANSPORTATION ALONG THE BLACK LINE.

   PUT THE PICTURES HERE (point) AND OUTLINE THEM
   IN YELLOW.

3. (Take all the pictures off the work page and spread them out on
   the table).

   (Say): PUT EACH PICTURE ON ITS OUTLINE.

           PASTE THE PICTURES IN PLACE.

"HIPPY" - Age 6 (1979)

Week: C
Activity: **Same-different (3)**

Work page (1)

(Say):
1. SHOW ME ALL THE FRAMES WITH TWO PICTURES THAT ARE DIFFERENT.
2. MARK THEM WITH AN X, AS IN THE EXAMPLE.

"HIPPY" - Age 6 (1979)

Appendix C

145

Work page (2)

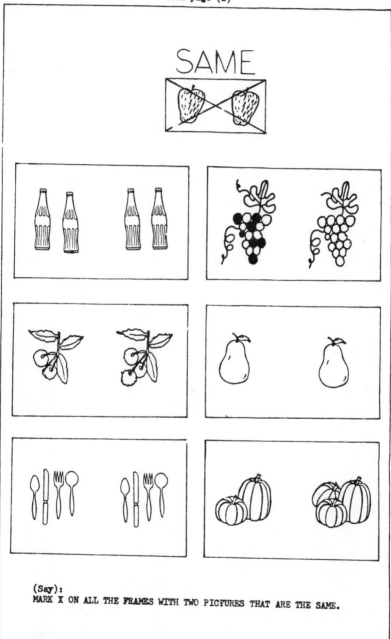

(Say):
MARK X ON ALL THE FRAMES WITH TWO PICTURES THAT ARE THE SAME.

"HIPPY" - Age 6 (1979)

Index

147

About the Author

Avima D. Lombard is a lecturer in early childhood education in the School of Education at The Hebrew University of Jerusalem. She is a senior researcher and research project director at the National Council of Jewish Women's Research Institute for Innovation in Education.

Dr. Lombard received the Ph.D. in education from the University of California, Los Angeles. She was assistant to the director of the UCLA Department of Education, where she served as evaluation coordinator of the Head Start Evaluation and Research Office. She has published articles in a number of journals in the field of early childhood education and is a member of several professional organizations in both the United States and Israel.